FREEDOM

Freedom is commonly recognised as the struggle for basic liberties, societies based upon open dialogue, human rights and democracy. The idea of freedom is central to Western ideas of modernity, but this engaging, accessible book argues that, if we look back at the history of the idea of freedom, then what we mean by it is far more contested than we might think. To what extent does freedom have a 'social' component, and how is it being reshaped by our dominant consumer society? This book represents a wake-up call to all those who thought our basic ideas of freedom were settled.

Today, the West sees itself as having a crucial role to play in exporting freedom into the far regions of the world – but our own freedom seems more under threat than ever. Linking ideas of public and personal freedom, Nick Stevenson explores complaints about Big Brother, the arrival of the business society and the erosion of democracy to show how our freedoms are far from secure.

Seeking to affirm the importance of freedom, this book provides a compelling argument for linking it to other values such as equality and responsibility. Drawing upon a range of critical thinkers and perspectives, Stevenson asks what freedom will come to mean in the future, in a world that seems increasingly fragile, uncertain and insecure.

Nick Stevenson is a Reader in Cultural Sociology at the University of Nottingham. He has written widely on questions of culture and politics. His published books include *The Transformation of the Media* (1999), *Making Sense of Men's Magazines* (2001), *Culture and Citizenship* (2001), *Understanding Media Cultures* (2002), *Cultural Citizenship* (2003), *David Bowie* (2006) and *Education and Cultural Citizenship* (2011).

SHORTCUTS – *'Little Books on Big Issues'*

Shortcuts is a major new series of concise, accessible introductions to some of the major issues of our times. The series is developed as an A to Z coverage of emergent or new social, cultural and political phenomena. Issues and topics covered range from Google to global finance, from climate change to the new capitalism, from blogs to the future of books. Whilst the principal focus of *Shortcuts* is the relevance of current issues, topics, debates and thinkers to the social sciences and humanities, the books should also appeal to a wider audience seeking guidance on how to engage with today's leading social, political and philosophical debates.

Series Editor: Anthony Elliott is a social theorist, writer and Chair in the Department of Sociology at Flinders University, Australia. He is also Visiting Research Professor in the Departments of Sociology at the Open University, UK, and University College Dublin, Ireland. His writings have been published in 16 languages, and he has written widely on, amongst other topics, identity, globalisation, society, celebrity and mobilities.

Titles in the series:

Confronting Climate Change
Constance Lever-Tracy

Feelings
Stephen Frosh

Suicide Bombings
Riaz Hassan

Web 2.0
Sam Han

Global Finance
Robert Holton

Freedom
Nick Stevenson

FREEDOM

Nick Stevenson

Routledge
Taylor & Francis Group

LONDON AND NEW YORK

First published 2012
by Routledge
2 Park Square, Milton Park, Abingdon, Oxon OX14 4RN

Simultaneously published in the USA and Canada
by Routledge
711 Third Avenue, New York, NY 10017

*Routledge is an imprint of the Taylor & Francis Group,
an informa business*

British Library Cataloguing in Publication Data
A catalogue record for this book is available from the British
Library

Library of Congress Cataloging in Publication Data
Stevenson, Nick.
Freedom / by Nick Stevenson.
v. cm. – (Shortcuts)
Includes bibliographical references and index.
Contents: Freedom now and then – Freedom and happiness – Big
brother and freedom – Cultural freedom – Cosmopolitan freedom
– Freedom and virtue.
1. Liberty. I. Title.
HM1266.S74 2012
322.44–dc23   2011034218

ISBN: 978-0-415-66449-3 (hbk)
ISBN: 978-0-415-66451-6 (pbk)
ISBN: 978-0-203-81880-0 (ebk)

Typeset in Bembo
by Taylor & Francis books

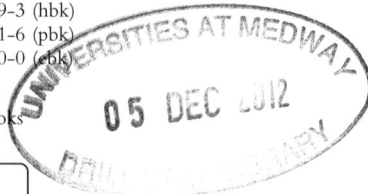

Printed and bound in Great Britain by
TJ International Ltd, Padstow, Cornwall

CONTENTS

Series Editor's preface   *viii*

1   Freedom now and then   1

2   Freedom and happiness   6

3   Big Brother and freedom   24

4   Cultural freedom   44

5   Cosmopolitan freedom   59

6   Freedom and virtue   71

Bibliography   *78*
Index   *82*

SHORTCUTS – *'Little Books on Big Issues'*

Series Editor's preface

Few topics are as politically urgent and theoretically complex as the search for freedom – which, as Nick Stevenson convincingly argues in this brilliant book, remains in our own time as fiercely contentious as ever. Both individuals and societies become truly free not when they dispense with constraint but when there is sufficient reflectiveness to meaningfully consider alternative ways of living – which is to underscore the very sense of freedom in choosing how to live. But it is precisely from this angle, according to Stevenson, that the sociological contradictions of freedom come to the fore: it is both blessing and curse, self-transformation and self-undoing. Ranging across popular culture, media, politics, cosmopolitanism and ethics, Nick Stevenson's *Freedom* is a wonderful shortcut not only for how we live now but how we might choose to live in the future.

Anthony Elliott

1

FREEDOM NOW AND THEN

Every civilised person today it seems is in favour of freedom. Freedom is commonly recognised as the struggle for basic liberties, societies based upon open dialogue, human rights and democracy. There are indeed global celebrities that signify the universal desire for freedom. The lives and passions of Nelson Mandela, the Dalai Lama and Aung San Suu Kyi are rightly recognised for the courageous role that they have played in the struggle for freedom. The images of these figures are recognised the world over as standing for the universal desire to live in liberty and freedom.

Indeed, as I write these words political commentators and newspaper columnists are eagerly discussing the Arab Spring where the cry for freedom is being heard across the Middle East. Despite the role the West has played supporting many of the authoritarian regimes in this region it now seems to want to play its part in the wider struggle for freedom. The West currently wishes to see itself as having a crucial role to play in exporting freedom into the far regions of the world from Burma to Libya and from China to Saudi Arabia. This is not surprising as the identity of the West is historically bound to the cause of freedom. However, if the promotion of freedom abroad is more complex than it might seem, there are obstacles to its realisation that also chime with the West's own internal history. Western societies remain hierarchical class-based societies ruled by elites who have historically used their power to limit the freedom of ordinary citizens. The story missing from the self-congratulatory talk about Western values is how these societies have sought to limit the freedom of the labouring classes, women, black people and others. The creation of internal hierarchies of rank, unemployment, job insecurity and poverty severely limit the experience of freedom of many ordinary citizens. Today, however, the dominant image of freedom for many in the West is of becoming wealthy and living a carefree life of consumption. This partly acts as a form of compensation for the anxiety and stress involved in earning a living in an increasingly competitive society.

But, as we shall see, there have been periods when ordinary citizens began to dream of more meaningful forms of freedom. This is indeed the story of the struggle for freedom from below by critical intellectuals and social movements. Active citizens did not reject the values of freedom because it did not seem to include them, but instead fought to make it meaningful in the context of their own lives. The struggle for freedom is not simply a story that takes place outside the frontiers of Western society, but just as crucially it is about the courageous struggle by many for a society where everyone (not just elites) can live lives of dignity, learning and fulfilment.

As will soon become apparent, I have chosen to focus upon debates in the context of the development of Western societies. In particular the relationship between Europe and North America is central to the story that I wish to tell. The idea of freedom has been central to the self-understanding of Western society and it is best understood as a narrative where citizens have struggled for rights and democratic societies. The desire for freedom usually means the desire to escape oppressive human societies and live in a more emancipated world. This is also central to any critical idea of sociology whose basic mission should be to throw light upon coercive institutions and help construct freer human societies. This is only possible if we have access to knowledge that can aid us in the process of reflection. In our current times sociology needs to become more closely aligned with the struggle for democratic institutions and public forms of reflection on questions of common concern. Of course not all of my fellow sociologists would share this view, but it remains an important strand within contemporary debates. Unless sociology can help us understand how the basic structures of human society have changed and how this can then be related to public questions and issues of how we might live then I am not sure what it is for.

In this mission I remain connected to the demands of the present and how freedom and democracy might be said to be currently under attack. This is not only through the development of a consumer society but also political ideologies that seek to downgrade a sense of shared civic identity. During the twentieth century, however, there were other periods, such as the 1930s (the rise of fascism, nationalism and mass unemployment), when democracy and freedom were more threatened than they are today. In discussing freedom and emancipation we need to keep a cool head and realise that the quest for freedom has had many twists and turns. Here we need some historical sense of those who claimed freedom in the past, as some of those who have shouted loudest for freedom have seen, at their journey's end, increasingly authoritarian societies. If there are no entirely free human beings there are certainly some societies that are freer than others. George Orwell's (1945) novel *Animal Farm* offers an instructive warning in this respect. History is full of cries for freedom that culminate less in emancipation than in new waves of submission, manipulation and control. What is particularly pressing about Orwell's account is that the bars of the prison are secured by jailors who continue to use the language of freedom. Orwell was particularly aware of how language could be perverted by authoritarian societies, which is why freedom requires democratic debate, criticism and a citizenry who are capable of thinking for themselves and who are independent-minded and never put their loyalty to their host society above the need for criticism. This is a hard call where many feel uncomfortable at being out of step with others and, not surprisingly, value security. But I believe that freedom is too important a value to be left to wither on the vine and that it is mostly the job of the political, media and education systems to make sure we are aware of its importance. There are grave dangers to freedom if the media is largely understood to be about entertainment or if education is largely just about the passing of exams. Journalists, educators, artists and social movements more generally have a special responsibility to keep alive the practice of freedom. We must learn to be critical.

Freedom really matters to me. As someone born into a poor but working family freedom was something that could only be won through courage, flexibility and collective endeavour. Schools were places where people like me learned to labour, the media was dominated by light entertainment and the workplace was mostly a space of dull compulsion. The question that emerges is, where in this setting could you learn about the possibilities of freedom? The labour movement, new social movements and more rebellious forms of popular culture such as punk and reggae had, it seemed to me, some of the answers. Freedom here became the struggle for an identity, questions that had no straightforward answers and the idea that the future was open. In particular the central educative message of the labour movement, that we should each have the possibility of discovering identities beyond the needs of our employers, is one to which I remain committed. Freedom appeared to me less as an abstract problem to be solved, and more of a concrete question as to how we should live.

Viewed historically, however, what becomes immediately apparent is that human societies could well have evolved without the idea. Ideas of freedom are not 'natural' but have been historically constructed. Sociologically, as Norbert Elias (1988) points out, for a society to survive it needs to organise an economy, control the means of violence and pass on knowledge. Without these essential features organised human societies would probably not last very long. If the citizens were starving, violence endemic and they had no understanding of themselves, then social and cultural collapse would not be far away. We could also say that the elites that control the economy, the military and the reproduction of knowledge are likely to find themselves in powerful positions. At this point Elias notes that during the twentieth century a political class sought to compete for power and organise the reproduction of society. The reader will note here that no mention is made of a free citizenry in the terms we understand because societies could well have evolved without them. While this story partially illustrates what an informed sociology might bring to these questions it also points to some of its limitations. If in the past sociology has spent too much time looking at how societies reproduce themselves or searching for laws of development, then the idea of freedom places new demands on the profession. Not only should sociology serve the practice of freedom, but it also needs to look at how and why it became meaningful in different social locations. In telling this story I have mainly relied upon the work of sociologists, but have also drawn from philosophers, political theorists and novelists. If we are to understand what freedom has become in our own time we need to draw upon a range of critical thinkers and perspectives. Yet, however we understand this story, we need to be clear that it might all have worked out differently.

2

FREEDOM AND HAPPINESS

In thinking about freedom it matters where you start. That we are members of a democratic society whose way of life is supposedly built upon self-governing institutions and the participation of ordinary citizens means that we value some freedoms more than others. However, most people, if asked, would say they wanted a happy life rather than a life spent participating in the meetings and committee arrangements necessary to make democracy work. Most people in this understanding would rather be happy than free. Yet I aim to argue that the not unproblematic or uncontested value of freedom has a central relevance for what might be broadly described as Western modernity. Here my argument is not that freedom is the only value or that it is relatively straightforward to understand or indeed that we can't live without it. There are other values like solidarity, equality or indeed happiness that are also important. And it is clearly mistaken to think that by virtue of being human we are free as this argument would not stand up to much historical scrutiny given the murderous, totalitarian and more generally repressive societies that have existed for the better part of human history. Part of the argument contained within this book is to convince the reader of the preciousness of freedom and how this definition has changed historically. We need to discover how freedom came to be taken for a value, and when it has been seen as something that people were willing to give their lives in order to defend. Further I also aim to argue that, in the context of Western modernity, while freedom is the source of intense disagreement, it should not be taken to simply mean anything. The debates about freedom have become pressing at some points in history rather than others, and our discussion needs to reflect this. Finally we need to look carefully at how freedom is being redefined today, and what the dangers might be.

Histories of freedom

In considering questions of freedom within the context of Western society there are some periods within which the issue was most intensely debated. We are still in the debt of these periods for delivering what many still regard as our central understandings of freedom. However, it is also important to consider more recent debates in respect of ideas of freedom, in particular the 1960s and the more recent period of neo-liberalism. Here part of my question is not only which definition of freedom should we value, but also how did it become a value? The historical sociologist Orlando Patterson (1991) argues that Western society only began to value freedom once it had experienced slavery. If we want to know who were the people who first valued being free, then we should look at slaves rather than philosophers. To be a slave in Ancient Greece was to experience a form of social death where your life literally was ruled by the will of another. Patterson argues that freedom became valued to the extent to which slavery was feared. To become a slave was to suffer a form of humiliation, though freedom was initially considered to be a feminine rather than a masculine value. Whereas an enslaved woman could dream of freedom in the future, such an option was not available for men. For men it was better to die than suffer the dishonour of slavery. Here, right at the beginning of Western ideas of freedom, we see that it begins life as the quest for personal freedom. The Greeks were later to turn the idea of freedom into a civic virtue whereby the good life was to be had through a life of self-reflection, dialogue with others and concern about questions of justice and the nature of the good. It was this way of life that was to become associated with democracies and seen as the opposite of a life of servitude. This idea of freedom is still with us today, but, from the beginning, freedom began life as an essentially sub-versive value that later ran the risk of being converted into a form of class distinction. In other words, as Patterson (1991) recognises, many of the Greek philosophers, such as Aristotle, argued that it was only those who were superior in knowledge who could be trusted with the capacity to rule. Freedom is not a purely emancipatory concept, but can be used to justified unfreedom elsewhere.

Following sociologist Zygmunt Bauman (1998), freedom is necessarily both a normative and an evaluative concept where we move from a subjugated to a better set of social conditions. But there is reason to believe that, as we ourselves become free, others may become less so. Freedom is a relational concept that suggests less the arrival of the perfect emancipated society than the desire to escape oppression. We need to remember that in the act of freeing ourselves we may do great harm to others. If, like in the case of the Greek slaves, the quest for freedom does not mean the arrival of society without any compulsion it should mean the arrival of a set of circumstances we might consider to be better.

The quest for freedom has never meant the desire for a society where everything becomes decided by entirely autonomous human beings. As Cornelius Castoriadis (1991) argues, for the most part we do not decide our language, culture, way of life or religion; these are largely decided for us by being a member of certain historical societies and communities rather than others. What matters is the extent to which members of society are encouraged to subject themselves and their social and cultural institutions to critical forms of thinking and analysis. It was the Greeks who discovered the possibility of instituting the autonomous society. Such a view has little to contribute as to whether such a society actually makes us happier (indeed it may make us more miserable). Here I can only say I am autonomous if I am capable of questioning myself as well as the laws that govern my community and wider society. Questions such as who am I and how ought I to live have an intrinsic relation to notions of freedom.

Similarly the political philosopher Hannah Arendt (1958) argues that freedom is a matter of being able to spontaneously introduce new pro-posals and practices into the public realm. For the Greeks freedom was unimaginable outside of a pluralistic public realm. There is no freedom without a public realm based upon the rule of law. We can define political tyranny as those governments that 'contradicted the essential human condition of plurality, the acting and speaking together, which is the condition of all forms of political organisation' (Arendt 1958: 202). Oppressive societies that disallow the possibility of human freedom impose isolation and fear upon the citizenry. A benevolent form of dictatorship may increase the well-being of the population but remains tyrannous if it does not allow for genuinely public forms of reflection, discussion and meeting.

If the Greeks are by and large responsible for historically creating the meanings that have become associated with Western freedom, then the European Enlightenment also contributed to that process. According to Tzvetan Todorov (2009), what mattered to the thinking of the European Enlightenment was the ability of individuals to decide for themselves as opposed to having to follow tradition. The Enlightenment was built upon the freedom to be able to think and to challenge established traditions. In particular Enlightenment intellectuals targeted religious forms of authority and argued in favour of the freedom of opinion and belief. Along with the development of science and rationality the Enlightenment gave birth to the idea that all humans should have universal rights. This inevitably restricts the autonomy of humans to do what they please and insists that human freedoms need to have certain limits. This meant that slavery would need to be abolished and that we should seek knowledge to free us from oppressive social and cultural conditions.

If, like the Greeks, however, the project for autonomy was built on the subjection of others the Enlightenment philosophers stopped short at criticising all forms of human domination. The historian George Mosse (1978) argues that, rather than considering racism as a footnote to the history of European thought, we should recognise its centrality. The new sciences of the Enlightenment and the concern to scientifically categorise 'man' in relation to 'nature' brought in an idea of the uncivilised barbarian. European freedom produced the idea of the primitive mind and the Other who required European forms of education and guidance. The idea of freedom, as we saw earlier, ends with the enslavement of non-European societies and was used to bolster self-satisfying ideas of European supremacy. Just as Greek ideas of freedom had been built upon the supremacy of the masters the same could be said of the European Enlightenment as it sought to keep 'inferior' races in a subordinate place.

Calls to freedom, as we shall see historically, are never innocent. They remain dependent upon an outside that most of our thinkers most of the time prefer not to acknowledge. Much of the writing on democracy prefers not to mention its more violent side and the crimes committed in its name. These questions can indeed be detected within the American and French revolutions that are often thought to be the political upheavals most associated with Enlightenment thinking. Hannah Arendt (1990) argued that the main difference between the two revolutions was that, whereas the American revolution was built upon the idea of freedom the French revolution ended in terror precisely because it failed to establish a stable republic based upon equal rights and representative institutions. For Arendt the French revolution and later the Russian revolution sacrificed political freedom to the desire to rid their own societies of want and poverty. This led Arendt to the pessimistic conclusion that the political attempt to tackle poverty and inequality would simply end in more repression. This, as we shall see, is an unnecessary argument, but Arendt is surely correct that one of the reasons that these revolutions faltered was because they failed to develop necessarily robust political institutions based upon civic freedoms. It was, paradoxically, revolutions driven by the welfare of the people that led to the destruction of freedom. We may also remember that the American revolution did indeed aim to create a society based upon the pursuit of happiness. Arendt (1990: 119) argues that this originally had a double meaning that included the possibility of a life of affluence, but also public forms of participation. Happiness in this context was not simply privatised leisure, but the pleasure involved in the public running their own communities and making their own laws. Arendt (1990: 127) argues that it was only later that happiness came to be located in private life as new waves of immigrants joined the republic seeking a life free from poverty.

The most celebrated observer of the American revolution was Alexis de Tocqueville. He is now most often remembered as an important contributor to a tradition of political thought called 'civic humanism'. As Charles Taylor (1989: 64) argues, such a model can be seen in stark distinction to modes of thought that can be connected to Rousseau and certain versions of Marxism. Civic humanism is critical of the idea that there could ever be a 'general will' that might be discovered by a particular class of intellectuals. Hence if Lenin emphasised the leading role of the Party in defining class consciousness then Rousseau emphasised the common will of the people. Totalitarian thought in the European context has waged war on the forms of human difference and plurality that accompanied democracy. If the idea of democracy sought to emphasise tolerance and compromise then we would need to recognise the legitimacy of different ideas of the good life. Totalitarianism by contrast sought to impose scientifically derived ideas of how humans may reach their full potential. The way to happiness and fulfilment was prescribed by state doctrine that required the violent submission of the host population. A free society is a plural society. Totalitarian societies sought to extinguish autonomy and replace it with an idea of a perfected humanity (Todorov 2003). This inevitably lead to the persecution of social and cultural groups who did not fit this model. It was the ability of the state to define happiness that led many critical intellectuals during the twentieth century to begin to fear the nightmare of the Big Brother society.

In civic humanism there is no common will or indeed general interest, but instead there are common political institutions, the rule of law, plural citizens and a participatory civic community. Tocqueville's (1998: 21) America charts the development of a civic way of life that seeks to draw together both 'well-being and liberty'. Tocqueville reported that civic participation had been built by dispersing the ownership of private property and establishing equal civic status through the granting of equal rights. Tocqueville observed how citizens participated through elected assemblies, town hall meetings and local assemblies. Such democratic assemblies had displaced wider distinctions of class and rank by providing spaces where citizens could generally mingle together. Tocqueville (1998: 204) noted that the flourishing of democratic and participatory communities had achieved what he called 'equality in freedom'. Further Tocqueville noted how complex webs of political association or civil society added to a broader sense of belonging and community amongst ordinary citizens. Freedom in Tocqueville's description depends upon a wider community of citizens who are willing to participate within political institutions and the running of their society more generally.

However Tocqueville duly notes that the rise of civic equality and democratic participation is threatened by the power of capital, anti-social individualism and of course slavery. American freedom and civic life was built upon brutal forms of oppression with 10 million African slaves being transported by 1820 (Keane 2009: 314). While the anti-slavery movement grew out of this contradiction it is true to say that the freedoms of the republic were built upon the oppression of black Africans. The freedoms we enjoyed (and to some extent continue to enjoy) came at a price.

Civic humanism offers a critique of Marxism through the explicit recognition of the plurality of freedom. Marxism imagined a life beyond conflict that will emerge once we recognise our common interest to end the domination of capitalism. Alternatively civic humanism emphasises that political communities are necessarily plural communities. Tocqueville also recognises that democracies can turn into tyrannous societies. This tends to happen if civic forms of participation and wider forms of association become undermined by individual forms of competition. Within democratic societies, as explicit definitions of rank tend to disappear (although class divisions remain), there is a considerable amount of anxiety about status. If your social standing was largely ascribed within aristocratic societies, then within a democratic order citizens are free to compete against one another in the bid to become 'better off' than their neighbours. This can lead society into an atomised state where citizens become increasingly free to ignore the authorities and can judge for themselves how they should live. Families tend to become the places of sacrifice and denial rather than the wider community. The ambiguity here is that if democratic citizenship offers the possibility of participation and equal rights this happens at a time when citizens become increasingly concerned with their private affairs (Poggi 1972). If the habits of democracy are largely applauded by Tocqueville as they give citizens an opportunity to exercise their judgement and to engage in the affairs of the wider society, then the broader sense of equal status encourages a shared anxiety that I could become as rich or as poor as anyone else (Offe 2005). The fault line of democracies is between individualism and civic association. Tocqueville was especially concerned that competitive individualism fashioned citizens who were indifferent to the past, future and current needs of their fellow citizens.

Despite civic humanism's critique of Marxism it remains important for its wider critique of capitalism. As Raymond Aron (1970) argues, Marxism persistently asks what is the importance of formal freedoms if everywhere is governed by employers and markets? When Aron asked this question in the 1960s he might be forgiven for thinking that liberal democracies had gone some way in linking personal and civic freedoms in a way that was preferable to that of state socialist societies. Here questions of well-being could be left to rising levels of prosperity and the development of social liberalism more generally. That such a solution is less convincing today will become apparent later.

Liberalism and freedom

If civic humanism makes explicit the importance of individual freedom, political community, equal civic status and participatory involvement, then more mainstream definitions of liberalism have preferred more individualistic accounts. John Stuart Mill's (1974: 59) classic work on liberty, written around the same time as Tocqueville, identified the central struggle of the age as between 'liberty and authority'. The key principle at stake in the safeguarding of freedom is the liberty of the individual that should only be limited to prevent harm. Mill was concerned not only with the coercive power of the state but with the freedom of individuals to come to their own conclusions without giving way to moral pressure from others. For this reason Mill (1974: 177) is rightly remembered not only as someone who argued that we are free to the extent to which we are not interfered with by others but as warning against the 'despotism of the mind'. By this Mill meant that democratic societies required awkward dissenting individuals who are unwilling to follow the crowd. Later Mill describes how his own tough-minded individualism would leave him feeling isolated from others. Here Mill recognises that what was missing was a sense of connection, community and sympathy with others. Mill (1924: 118) argues this offered him 'no delight in virtue, or the general good'. Indeed it was the experience of a deep depression that led Mill to conclude that to focus too inwardly upon your own happiness leads only to misery; it is better to involve yourself in projects that served the well-being of others. However, it also awakened within Mill (1924: 121) the idea that the freedom of the individual was not only an external question but also concerns 'the internal culture of the individual'. Freedom was not only a matter concerning the lack of external constraint, but living a life of felt connection to others, and cultivating the self.

Isaiah Berlin's (1959) equally renowned defence of negative liberty as the capacity to choose without interference from others took its lead from Mill. The basic freedom for Berlin is to be found in our capacity to choose between different alternatives. The problem with what Berlin had identified as 'positive freedom' was that it imposed upon members of the community a substantive conception of the good. The best way to live your life could only be decided by individuals and never the broader society. This essay, originally delivered as a lecture in 1958, was widely interpreted as a critique of totalitarianism, given the lack of civic freedoms that were able to flourish in state-dominated societies. Read more closely, however, Berlin links the importance of personal freedom and civic freedoms, as opposed to the coercion used by more authoritarian regimes who aim to reveal the 'true nature' of men and women. Freedom and happiness were best lived individually and should not be collectively defined. But Berlin was writing in an era of social liberalism where freedom could not simply be understood as formal freedom; it also required a degree of equality. Berlin wondered what use was freedom in the context of grinding poverty or social injustice? What is missing from both Mill and Berlin is a more careful consideration of the kinds of democratic community that will allow freedom to flourish. Both Mill and Berlin (despite their insights) are overly reliant upon individualistic accounts of freedom that disallow the civic humanist emphasis upon the interactions of plural beings in public spaces. As Arendt (1961) has argued, ideas of negative liberty have their basis in Christianity's concerns about free will. Here freedom becomes associated with freedom from constraint whereas civic humanism seeks to emphasise the collective and societal basis of freedom. Freedom is less being left to our own devices and more about requiring the construction of common institutions.

The view of freedom defended by Mill and Berlin is sometimes called 'negative freedom' or the idea we are free to the extent to which we are not constrained. Charles Taylor (1991) argues that negative freedom has too little to say about self-determination. Can we really say that we are personally free just because we are not externally constrained? What of those who are fearful, have low personal esteem or are inhibited in other ways? More explicitly Taylor means to identify an ethic which can be traced back to the Romantics that we become free by the extent to which we are true to ourselves and can live authentic lives. Here I can be said to be living a dignified life to the extent to which I follow a path of my own choosing and a calling of my own. There are then higher human goals than simply being happy.

These ideas have been most explicitly given expression in what is an overlooked book in the context of the discussions of freedom. The most systematic attempt to link personal freedom and participation within a democratically defined community can be found within Erich Fromm. Fromm (1941) argued that, while a liberal culture of rights and external freedoms was an important advance upon previous societies, we need also to consider inner restraints. Fromm wished to point out that the task of becoming yourself was more difficult than it might at first appear. How can I be sure that the person I have become is not simply to please others (usually parents) or to gain access to the dominant symbols of success in an increasingly consumer-driven society? Missing from much mainstream liberal thought has been the idea that freedom may become overrun and corrupted by the market. Indeed, Fromm (1995) argues that the idea of 'living as easy' is a recent invention of an overtly consumerist age. That freedom requires little from us is perhaps not surprising in a society where huge numbers of people can 'get what they want' by entering a supermarket. That the question of who we should become is profoundly difficult and is not something many people at present wish to hear. Are we 'free' if our opinions are handed to us by a capitalist-run media, our ideas fit in with current fashions, and we simply aim to make our perspectives acceptable to others? Indeed, can citizens experience themselves as free if they see themselves less as citizens with civic identities but as politically powerless, disenfranchised and fearful? In particular Fromm was concerned that such features could be linked to a latent authoritarianism whereby citizens sought to follow powerful leaders rather than form their own opinions. Fromm is describing the condition of unfreedom as a subtle form of slavery where the burden of freedom is too great and it is easier to conform to mainstream ideas and beliefs. Citizens invest in powerful and undemocratic leaders as a way of compensating themselves for their own internally felt lack of significance. Here, as Fromm (1941: 177) puts it, 'one gains security, against the torture of doubt'.

However the emphasis upon the idea of personal freedom as self-determination played an important part in the redefinition of liberalism. Paul Starr (2007) argues that as liberalism has developed it has progressively taken on ideas of self-development and has moved beyond a purely negative conception of freedom. Here liberalism calls for greater state intervention into the economy to reduce inequality, develop a welfare state and provide access to education. If the liberalism of the eighteenth century primarily concerned freedom, as opposed to a conservative emphasis upon tradition, then in the twentieth century it became identified with the right to develop the self. This not only meant tackling inequality and poverty but the possibility of higher standards of living for the majority as well as access to education more generally. In particular the 1960s saw the re-emergence of the idea of self-development being linked to notions of the democratic community. Here we might point to the rise of a democratic idea where the free development of the self was linked to that of the community. This offered a political vision that is close to civic humanism but that goes beyond individualistic liberalism and classical Marxism. If, as Fromm argues, authoritarianism and the fear of freedom had its roots within the self and a sense of powerlessness, then what kind of democratic community could be developed to address these questions?

The long revolution and freedom

At this point I want to introduce Raymond Williams's idea of the long revolution.

More easily placed in a tradition of post-war democratic socialism, Williams's idea explicitly sought to create the conditions of an 'educated democracy and a common culture' for everyone (Williams 1965: 176). Like many democratic socialists of his time Williams saw the development of the 'social state' as a means of promoting a more 'civilised' and democratic human society. However, Williams makes a distinctive contribution in that he did not merely seek to utilise state power to promote a good society, but sought to democratise the state while promoting the conditions for common forms of cultural engagement. In other words, Williams was as concerned with social welfare as he was with questions of public freedom. To understand this we have to take seriously his writing on questions of culture.

For Williams, ideas of 'culture' are not simply to be contrasted to a debased mass society. Questions of culture matter because they help to define the very process of learning and the transformation of identity within contemporary society. Rather than simply defending certain works of 'civilisation' Williams emphasises the public role that mass communication, art, education and popular culture might play within modern society. In doing this, he describes the struggle for a learning and communicative society as the long revolution (Williams 1965). Human beings are creative and communicative beings capable of offering new experiences, perceptions and ways of seeing to the wider community. For Williams (1962: 47) 'the artist, in this case, is not the lonely explorer, but the voice of his community'. Art, on this reading, serves the cause of freedom as it remains related to common practices of interpretation evident in ordinary forms of communication. That we are all capable of redescribing our society and sharing meanings means that our education, media and other cultural systems need to be democratised as far as possible. Our freedom finds expression within our capacity to find new and imaginative ways of communicating with each other.

These ideas have a marked family resemblance to the civic republican tradition. Yet, unlike Arendt, Williams is seeking to discover a society where we all might flourish while participating in an energetic civil society built upon autonomous and above all creative forms of cultural production. For Williams (1965: 10) the democratic revolution could be said to be 'at a very early stage'. Despite the development of mass literacy, the prospect of participating in democratic elections, new communications technology and labour organisations, society remained dominated by the needs of capitalism. Only the gradual emergence of a complex democratic and socialist society could give full expression to the individual's capacity to be creative, autonomous and live a more fully realised life. To do this we need to create a culture in common. For Williams (1989) a culture in common had several aspects, but overall it was an instituted culture of dialogue rather than agreement. To be able to talk of a culture in common meant rejecting the choice between either atomised privatisation or cultural communalism. Freedom meant the development of democratic public spaces of engagement built upon a shared education system that had broken with the class-bound logic of the past. The *common* element of Williams's argument concerns the ability of ordinary people – not just paid professionals – to contribute, criticise and reinterpret aspects of their culture. Within this process the meanings of 'high' or indeed 'popular' culture are not fixed in stone but require open criticism by members of the community. Notably Williams provides a defence of the ability of literature and drama to ask critical questions of both historical and more contemporary societies. In this respect, complex works of art and criticism did not belong solely to the dominant class, but could be commented on potentially by everyone. For Williams democratic socialism remains connected to the capability of citizens to learn through the education system, creative engagement and democratised public spheres. Later Williams would describe socialism as 'not only the general "recovery" of specifically alienated human capacities, but also, and much more decisively, the necessary institution of new and very complex communicative capacities and relationships' (Williams, 1980: 62). Democratic socialism is related to the empowerment of trade unions, the development of a democratised society and a participatory polity that overwhelmingly depends upon the recovery of voice. For Williams capitalism had little interest in developing the critical and creative potential perspectives of the vast majority of the population, preferring instead vocationalism in education, commercial forms of television and uncritical forms of mass consumption. In particular Williams explained how powerful elites had historically held onto power by maintaining the class system and failing to develop a critical media and education system.

The idea of 'the long revolution' offers an answer to the question of what a good society and a good life might be. The answer that Williams gave was a place where ordinary people could become creative, be actively involved in the key decisions that were made in their society and develop themselves through education (Rustin 2007a). The long revolution as the learning society had to be permanently open to the challenge of new voices and perspectives, and in this respect would in more contemporary times have had to adopt a more self-consciously multicultural vocabulary. However, the long revolution was unlikely to progress much further unless the labour movement could radically transform capitalism and institute a genuinely democratic society.

Postmodernism and neo-liberalism

What then has happened to the idea of freedom contained within Raymond Williams's idea of the long revolution? Why has our faith evaporated in the dream of a society where citizens progressively become free as they develop themselves, participate within a democratised society and learn through education, art and the public sphere to think critically? The first answer concerns an enhanced scepticism concerning the idea of freedom more generally on the part of social movements. If feminism, black politics and gay liberation at the end of the 1960s were initially interested in redefining freedom, this has recently been thrown into doubt. Postmodern thought more generally has steadily abandoned liberal ideas of freedom and become progressively interested in criticising dominant discourses. To understand this philosophical shift we need to understand the impact that post-structuralism and postmodern philosophy has had on the human sciences and the humanities. There has been a sustained critique of Enlightenment-based forms of understanding that offer the idea that human freedom emerges through our ability to enter into dialogue with each other and to ask critical questions. In the first place, the criticism argues, such a disposition is not the 'essence' of being human as some Enlightenment philosophers argued, but is better seen as a historically defined event. In other words, the Enlightenment does not take us any closer to 'the truth' but merely registers a shift in our shared cultural conventions. The philosopher Michel Foucault (1984a), who has profoundly influenced this way of thinking, argues that we should try and refuse what he calls the 'blackmail' of the Enlightenment. This is where we are autonomous rational beings or we are trapped in the confines of tradition. Instead it is better that we understand ourselves as children of the Enlightenment who have been instructed in how we ought to be. The paradox of Enlightenment thinking is that we have been 'instructed' to be free and to think of ourselves as rational beings. The Enlightenment has offered us direct instructions on how to be free. This programme, as we have already seen, was far from innocent given that it contained categories of people who were unable to live up to its image. Foucault is suggesting that in offering an image of freedom as rational and disinterested thinking it ended up creating an Other. The Other of the ability to be able to use reason at various points historically might be said to be the colonised, women, people of different sexual orientations and the working-class population more generally.

This way of thinking has encouraged social movements to give up asking how might we become free. The fear is that, once freedom becomes codified and normalised, this ends in the creation of new Others and outgroups who are unwilling (or unable) to live up to the new dominant norms. To ask how might we be free risks judging others seen as being incapable of living up to this definition. If our images of freedom are dominated by educated middle-class people, then we might become intolerant of those who are poor, break the law and seem less than virtuous. However, we might also argue that this cultural disposition does not so much give up on the idea of human freedom but instead radicalises it in important ways.

Notably in Michel Foucault's (1984b) final work he returns to the Greeks in pursuit of a different understanding of human freedom. Here Foucault offers a very different idea of Greek thought to that of Arendt. Instead of the emphasis placed upon freedom as a means of participating within a plural public, Foucault stresses the cultivation or care of the self. This was a way of educating the self in terms of how we might wish to live and of learning to please ourselves. The ethical sensibility uncovered by Foucault is a form of radical individualism that avoids domestication (no universal laws as to how others might live) but instead experiments with what one might become. Such a position is probably very easy to dismiss as being the product of narcissistic self-absorption. However, Foucault was convinced that there could be a considerable growth in human freedom if we are creative with our identities and give up on the need to live consistently within certain categories. Freedom here becomes the capacity of the self to engage in questions of reinvention without requiring the certainty of belonging to a definite 'category'. As we give up on the need to fit ourselves into fixed categories the self is experienced as more plural, open and creative.

The problem with this argument is that it rejects all universal thinking as domestication. The idea of human rights becomes suspicious as it promotes human universals that allow us to criticise some societies rather than others. The linking together of human rights and democracy are human universals that can be defended on the grounds of increasing human freedom both inside and outside the West. Missing from postmodernism more often than not is an idea as to why we might prefer democratic forms of reflection to more authoritarian societies. While social movements are rightly concerned with the domestication of Otherness they should be equally concerned about the closing down of critical public spaces where alternative sensibilities and lifestyles can become interrogated and criticised. Such a view inevitably moves us back to concerns about human plurality, autonomy and democracy, all of which are Enlightenment concerns.

If postmodern forms of thinking have to some extent led to a displacement of more democratic modes of reflection this has been less important than the development of neo-liberalism. In brief, neo-liberalism is an aggressive form of capitalism that is hostile to organised labour and the welfare state, while seeking to privatise public goods, cut taxes and promote a climate favourable to business (Harvey 2005). Neo-liberalism as the dominant form of politics since the 1980s has sought to resignify freedom as market freedom. Pierre Bourdieu (2003: 29) argues that neo-liberalism is far from culturally neutral given its attempts to deregulate the labour market, promote casual and insecure forms of employment, overwork and consumer-orientated lifestyles. In particular, neo-liberalism promotes a world of inequality between poly-cultural cosmopolitan elites and the poor, who increasingly take refuge in reactive forms of nationalist politics. Whereas the main political parties seek to present their actions as sensible reactions to global pressures they actually pursue 'a policy of depoliticisation' (Bourdieu 2003: 38). In this context, the danger is that the rule of money and power will seek to downgrade artistic works, education, media and the relative autonomy of culture from the market. If we bring the increasing dominance of neo-liberalism together with postmodernism we can perhaps see why civic republicanism and the more radical ideas of the long revolution have been swept aside.

Freedom and happiness

If the idea of freedom has become market freedom under neo-liberalism it is noticeable that many on the political Left have become more interested in questions of happiness. The relatively high levels of political engagement, social solidarity and well-being experienced by previous generations have been gradually undermined by an increasingly competitive society (Hamilton 2004; Layard 2005). More recently there has been other evidence to suggest that unequal societies (especially given the status competition that they engender) lead not only to increased mental ill-health but also to a range of other social ills from teenage pregancy to obesity and from poor educational performance to violence (Wilkinson and Pickett 2009). A society based upon well-being requires a shared sense of social solidarity and equality that has been undermined by market societies. At heart most of these studies offer an under-standing of citizens not as individuals seeking to maximize freedom, but as social creatures that mostly gain a sense of well-being through their immediate ties to their families and local communities. Indeed the spirit of Tocqueville is evident in Robert Putnam's (2000) account of an increasingly atomised social landscape where citizens have lost a sense of civic virtue and withdrawn into the home and away from participation within their communities. All of these studies are valuable in that they offer a critique of the rise of privatised lifestyles and the decline in parti-cipation within civic and voluntary organisations. This in turn has led to greater social isolation and a breakdown in trust and social solidarity more generally. Taken together these studies offer an alternative vision to a dominant politics that offers more privatisation, inequality, consumerism and lives of fearful uncertainty. The argument here is that, if citizens felt able to participate in the act of making communities, then they would live more fulfilled and happier lives. The reason that this has become so difficult is the rise of home centredness, growing numbers of citizens working longer hours and the development of increasing inequalities between rich and poor. If the 1960s feared the robotic society that robbed citizens of their individuality, then in more recent times it is social atomism and withdrawal from the life of the community that is attracting most concern.

While significant and striking, however, some of this work suffers from being overly utilitarian in focus. As Michael Rustin (2007b) has argued, the idea of 'the greatest happiness to the greatest number' does not really offer a complex language of how we might decide the best way to live. Indeed many of the happiness studies seem to suggest that if only we could get off the 'hedonic treadmill' we could all start living happier, more community-oriented and fulfilled lives. While the argument stops short of the programmes for happiness that were evident within totali-tarian societies, it fails to recognise that we live in a society where there are plural understandings of the good life. Here we would do well to remind ourselves of Charles Taylor's (1982) critique of utilitarian ethics. For Taylor utilitarianism has the capacity to do great damage to the complexity of our lives. It does this by reducing complex moral and ethical questions to calculations for the happiness of the majority. For example, if we take the idea of freedom we have been discussing, then we can see just how important this has been in the history of Western society. To live in freedom has been taken to have a personal meaning in terms of living your own life and passionately pursuing goals of your own choosing. This has meant the struggle for a society where we are able to democratically participate in the running of our communities. Arguably this moral source continues to be a powerful source within contemporary societies and is perhaps just as important as the desire to be happy.

Indeed I doubt that the need for modern people to lead happy lives is as important as the need for us to live creatively and meaningfully. Victor Frankl (1964) has written that the aim of life is not a life of contented happiness but how we shoulder the burden of living and the meanings that can become attached to it. We act morally not because we live in communities that have been designed to make us happy, but because we have an inner sense of purpose that gives meaning to our lives. There is then no meaningful life without frustration, complexity and difficulty. The introduction of ideas of human freedom into the debate about happiness has profound consequences as to how we understand the questions at stake. Here we should be careful in case the argument becomes the need to replace atomised competitive lives with ones that are more equal and communally oriented no matter how desirable this might seem. Victor Frankl's insights offer us a different starting place, which is that each human being is charged with the need to discover the purpose of their lives. The quest to decide who we are, how we are tied to history and how best to become ourselves is of course not a purely individual question. If we are indeed to live meaningfully then everyone needs the opportunity to become themselves. This, as we shall see, was an idea shared by George Orwell, one of the most important writers on freedom.

3

BIG BROTHER AND FREEDOM

If freedom is both a public and private value, then its opposite was perhaps most graphically imagined by George Orwell. It is Orwell's novel *Nineteen Eighty-Four* that is most often returned to by the liberal imagination as offering the nightmare vision of unfreedom. Indeed, Orwell should be remembered not only as a politically committed writer, but also as one who scorned the hedonistic life and valued above all our shared capacity for dissent. The complaints about a Big Brother society are most often from citizens whose lives are under surveillance, who are denied basic liberties, misinformed by the media or too fearful to lead the lives of their choosing. Big Brother of course can come in many guises and can be anything from the repressive arm of the state, or complaints about corporate power, to more personal forms of intimidation from women too frightened to go out alone at night or workers afraid to join trade unions. The Big Brother society is the control society. Such is the centrality of this metaphor to Western ideas of freedom we have to perhaps remind ourselves that it was originally thought up in quite different social and cultural circumstances to the ones that persist today. The novel, as we shall see, was clearly written as a warning and was never really intended to act as an accurate description of reality. Here I want to return to George Orwell's vision and argue that with good reason it remains central to our quest to understand freedom.

George Orwell is sometimes remembered as a conservative writer, elitist and intellectual of the Cold War. These are of course simplifications for someone whose life and writing stands as a testimony to the importance of freedom. Orwell is best remembered as a complex individual who recognised the importance of the hidden politics of empire and the nation state and that freedom is a precious value that is often entangled with the enslavement of others (Orwell 1968a). In terms of Orwell's critical legacy he has undoubtedly suffered at the hands of those like E.P. Thompson (1978) who are critical of Orwell's pessimism in respect of the possibilities of radical politics. Thompson is particularly critical of those who used Orwell as a means of promoting conformism in respect of the politics of the Cold War and losing the possibilities of a more emancipated society. A conservative class of intellectuals had followed Orwell in dispensing the politics of the good society for the containment of the 'evil' of communism. Indeed, it is true that Orwell's attitude to his fellow intellectuals was often scornful and this added to a deep-seated pessimism regarding the possibilities of avoiding a future totalitarian society, making him an ambivalent figure. Yet Orwell (1968b: 571) was deeply critical of intellectuals who liked to stay 'inside the whale' where it is 'very comfortable, cosy, homelike' and those who merely conformed to the orthodoxy of the prevailing ideologies of the time. It is also true that in this Orwell was deeply sensitive to the failings of socialists rather than those on the political right; however, what also needs to be remembered is Orwell's recognition that it was the responsibility of the intellectual to 'tell truth to power'. Like Edward Said (1994: 71) Orwell believed that intellectuals had a special responsibility not to overlook the crimes of their own political side or their nation state. Orwell was an important intellectual given his commitment to questions of truth and honesty and his ability to locate himself within a particular intellectual tradition (democratic socialism) while being critical of those who indulged in intellectual evasions and easy answers. Edward Said (1994: 73) in a similar spirit argues that intellectuals have a duty to address the ways in which power had become constituted in their own society and to address 'programs of discrimination, repression, and collective cruelty'. It is this George Orwell I would wish to recover. Despite the way that Orwell has been used by the political Right as a Cold War ideologist contrasting the freedoms of the liberal West as opposed to the repressive life of the Eastern bloc, he remained a democrat and a socialist. We should then read Orwell's (1999) great novel *Nineteen Eighty-Four* less as a diatribe against socialism and more as a warning of the dangers of authoritarianism. Orwell wrote later:

> My recent novel is NOT intended as an attack on Socialism or the British Labour Party (of which I am a supporter) but as a show up of the perversions to which a centralised economy is liable and which have already been partly realised in Communism and Fascism. I do not believe that the kind of society I describe *will* arrive, but I believe (allowing of course for the fact that the book is a satire) that something resembling it *could* arrive.
>
> *Orwell (1968c: 502)*

The novel, which is still part of the public imagination, offers a nightmare vision of a possible future society. Winston Smith, the main protagonist, is an outsider in a world of suspicion, state domination, continual surveillance and human cruelty. The control of the central Party embodied through the presence of Big Brother should be read as the personification of the anti-democratic society. Personal and public freedom has disappeared as there are no spaces left not entirely controlled by telescreens that are used to disseminate propaganda and to spy upon individual citizens. If the division of public and private has been erased by constant surveillance so has the public ability to speak authentically within the public realm given the dominance of lies manufactured by the central Party. It is only a dispirited working-class population (the proles) who are viewed as too politically insignificant to be placed under the watchful eye of telescreens. Here the thoughts and behaviour of the 'educated' population are constantly being monitored for signs of dissent. In particular the novel makes much of the Party's ability to be able to remanufacture the past and to pervert the English language by gradually replacing complex words and meanings with a more instrumental language. The constant deluge of propaganda is only interrupted by regular doses of hatred against 'the enemy' Goldstein. The ideological control of the population emerges through the constant surveillance to nullify oppositional ideas and disseminate 'positive' propaganda and, perhaps the most significant of all, fear and hatred. The fact that Oceania is constantly at war with an external enemy and the requirement that Party members engage in periodic bursts of hatred against internal and external Others means that everyday life is infused with fear and paranoia. Prominent themes throughout the narrative are: who can be trusted not to betray you? Are you 'seen' as patriotic enough? And who is watching you?

If the architecture of the novel is well-known, what is important in our context is the vision of a state-dominated world that manufactures lies and has extinguished civil society. Conformity is guaranteed by the threat of liquidation, the fear of being reported for a thought crime, propaganda and the elimination of any meaningful opposition. The principles of Newspeak eliminate words with oppositional meanings while 'doublethink' is capable of inverting meanings. The Ministry of Truth tells continual lies, the Ministry of Peace promotes war and the Ministry of Love seeks to outlaw sexuality and promote law and order.

Much of the middle section of the book is caught up with the love affair between Smith and Julia. The extremely militarised and hyper-masculinised state cannot allow for ordinary feelings of human reciprocity and tenderness. Here Orwell partially recognises how a cruel and mas-culinised society seeks to drive out compassionate and loving human relations. As bell hooks (2004) argues, if patriarchy in its most extreme formations celebrates a form of hyper-masculinity, it does so by closing down alternatives and by instituting rule through naked power, fear and the repression of feelings. The militarised and masculine state elim-inates both public and more personal forms of freedom. Ultimately this is a world without a sense of trust or what Orwell calls 'common decency' (Crick 2007: 151). A civic participatory culture is disabled in a world of fear, mutual suspicion and lack of fellow feeling. Freedom is a fragile plant: it can sometimes grow within cracks in the concrete, but more often it needs a liberal culture that honours dissenting points of view and a capacity to take responsibility for the well-being of our fellow citizens.

In the final stages of the novel Winston Smith is tortured by O'Brien and is finally led to enter room 101 where he has to face his greatest fear. It is at this point that Smith's resistance to the will of the Party and Big Brother is finally broken and he is allowed to go back to work after he has been successfully reprogrammed. The most terrifying aspect of the novel's final stages is Orwell's argument that there is no possibility of resistance against totalitarian systems rooting out all opposition and finally transforming the most intransigent into compliant men and women. Winston Smith reflects

> But they could get inside you. 'What happens here is forever', O'Brien had said. That was a true word. There were some things, your own acts, from which you could not recover. Something was killed in your breast: burnt out, cauterised out.
>
> *(Orwell 1999: 229)*

Here the politics of totalitarian dominance seeks not only to control thoughts and reality, but becomes intoxicated with power and human cruelty. Individual forms of dissent are stamped on and eradicated. There is, it seems, no limits to the power of the state and Party machinery as O'Brien remarks, '[I]f you want a picture of the future, imagine a boot stamping on a human face – forever' (Orwell 1999: 211). The hyper-masculinised world of Big Brother is a world that has eliminated the possibility of disorder and unpredictability and has done so by converting the population into a controllable and manipulable mass. The fascist society imagined by Orwell is built upon masculine toughness and the elimination of self-criticism, ambiguity and more empathetic feelings.

The novel was completed towards the end of Orwell's life and is overshadowed by a profound sense of paranoia. Having survived the fighting in the Spanish civil war, the end of the Second World War and the death of his wife, Orwell's own life was coming to a close. Many have commented that there is a marked similarity between the brutality of *Nineteen Eighty-Four* and Orwell's (1953) own experiences of the English public school system (fear, bullying, inhumanity and forced rote learning). Orwell's writing at this point might be understood as seeking to explore the pedagogy of totalitarianism. Like Hannah Arendt (2000) totalitarian domination is understood as a fanatical form of power that sought to replace human plurality with a manipulated mass public. For both Orwell and Arendt freedom was less about the defence of an autonomous individual and more concerned with the defence of plural publics. Orwell (1968d: 160) writes that the 'greatest mistake is to imagine the human being is an autonomous individual. The secret freedom which you can supposedly enjoy under a despotic government is nonsense, because your thoughts are never entirely your own.' The practice of freedom requires a dialogic context where we can exchange different ideas and debate different positions. It is precisely these practices that are threatened by power rather than freedom.

James Decker (2004) describes Orwell's dystopian novel as offering a post-ideological account. By this he means that all opposition and ideological contestation have been systematically eliminated. This is a totalitarian world as there are no counter-ideologies and forms of resistance that are not ultimately complicit with the rule of Big Brother. Such a view has a similarity with other accounts of Western modernity that can be found in some works of critical theory. Herbert Marcuse (1972) argued that by the 1960s so-called liberal democracies had become capitalist and technologically dominated one-dimensional societies. The manipulated society had achieved 'euphoria in unhappiness' (Marcuse 1972: 19). A more up-to-date example similar to Marcuse's own might be traced through the development of positive psychology that is now regularly used by commercial enterprises to help employees foster 'the right' attitudes towards their lives. Positive psychology encourages workers to dispel all negative thoughts about themselves and to be optimistic, future orientated and above all happy (Ehrenreich 2010). Happy smiling workers are less likely to fall ill, be unproductive or even start agitating for a different less unequal and unfair society. These ideas have not surprisingly taken hold in increasingly market-dominated societies driven by profit, competiveness and the need to look after number one. The issue here is not to champion negativity, but to recognise how such overt attempts at thought control might be justifiably described as Orwellian in their implications, and are driven by the needs of a capitalist economy. Should you fail to get the job, enhance your performance or achieve the promotion you were looking for, then it is probably your fault for not being 'positive' enough. Clearly this detracts a considerable amount of attention away from more critical ideas about capitalism and the market economy, and demonstrates why the economic system in terms of education has tended to focus upon vocational courses as opposed to the critical development of citizens. This points to a different ideology to that which seeks to manufacture compliance. Rather than seeking to produce pro-market identities, the other means by which market societies operate is to systematically fail to develop a critical rather than a merely functional literacy amongst the population. Many of capitalism's poorer citizens have been branded 'educational failures'. Citizens through a lack of political will or resources (or a combination of the two) have received only the most basic education. The ability to be able to 'read the world' critically is necessary for any meaningful definition of citizenship.

Like Orwell, Marcuse (1972) is concerned about the dominance of a society based upon a form of totalitarian manipulation that has effectively eliminated more authentic forms of critical reflection. This has been brought about in the context of an affluent society where we are no longer able to separate true and false needs and oppositional forms of politics are quickly incorporated back into the system. Here, like Orwell, I think that Marcuse's polemic might be usefully read as arguing less that our society is actually like this but more that liberal democratic societies both carry totalitarian aspects within them and are capable of cancelling democratic ways of life. Further, that, whereas Orwell concentrates on state-dominated societies, the market is equally capable of fixing certain ideas and concepts into people's heads and this prevents the emergence of a more critical questioning attitude amongst the public more generally.

Orwell is a profoundly important figure in the story of freedom as he was able to imagine what a society of unfreedom might be like. Indeed, many state-controlled countries today either actively repress his writing or find it a source of profound embarrassment. However, such is the crudity of the society described in Orwell's novel we might be forgiven for thinking it has little to tell us about the politics of a complex, information-based society. Much of the time the claim we are living in the age of Big Brother is a complaint about the reduction of civil liberties and the increased ability of the state to monitor the population. As important as these questions are, however, the threat of Big Brother is also concerned with a politics of thought control and a repressive and cruel state. Orwell's legacy is of course to remind us about the power of the state, but also to awaken us to the possibility of thought control and the attempt to manufacture a complicit citizenry. Here the central question I want to ask is, to what extent are modern mediated societies capable of such control and ideological fixity rather than democratic discussion and a civic debate? The Big Brother figure of *Nineteen Eighty-Four* remains significant for our time not as an anti-communist weapon but as a means of awakening issues of ideological control that are central to any meaningful definition of freedom.

The new media age?

The idea that culture has become more rather than less ideologically contested is the dominant position amongst many who study the media today. This argument suggests that if old media was built upon the flow of information from centre to periphery it has been radically reconstructed in the new media age. The development of new technological forms, such as computers, mobile phones and iPods, could be said to have 'empowered' citizens by the extent to which they have enabled them to become producers of cultural texts and not just consumers. The development of more lateral forms of mediated communication through the production of blogs, Facebook, Twitter and alternative websites means that the communicative power of civil society has been considerably enhanced since the days when cultural communication was largely governed by one-way 'old' media such as television and the press. This should mean that states find the media more difficult to control given its multifarious and complex nature. Indeed, if in the past many radical critics complained that old style media led to the passivity of its citizens this can no longer be assumed to be the case given the popular rise of two-way media that potentially opens the possibility of enhanced forms of democratic dialogue. Earlier generations of radical media critics sought to argue that the development of new technology could have emancipatory implications. This is less an age of totalitarian dominance than a noisy public sphere full of different perspectives and citizen–journalists.

Manuel Castells, whose earlier work has sought to investigate the contours of an emergent informational order, more recently comes close to endorsing a similar position. If the Orwellian universe was fearful of a powerful state the network society has witnessed a growth in the ability of social movements organised by citizens to interrupt the agendas of ruling cosmopolitan elites. Castells's recent work continues on this theme by arguing that the network society is both global and vertically organised through the Internet. If capitalism has become more firmly entrenched than ever then 'resistance identities have exploded' (Castells 2009: 37). The network society is not built upon homogeneity but precisely the opposite as relatively autonomous networks seek to foster a complex global civil society. The development of grassroots organisations on the Web as well as the development of social messaging has greatly expanded the power of civil society. The Internet in terms of civil society offers fewer hierarchical structures and the potential of more inclusive forms of public space. This has subsequently enabled the development of the citizen–journalist (that is someone who is both a citizen and who can make a cultural contribution by writing a blog or developing a website).

Such features can also be seen as a shift from more traditional forms of class politics toward more lifestyle and global questions on the part of some activists. The Internet brings together local and global problems and enables citizens to become not only the consumers of information but producers as well. Henry Jenkins (2004) has argued that despite the increasing domination of corporations within the culture industry globally, networked media allows new sites for popular forms of resistance and for creative forms of cultural production. If fans of popular culture in the past were marked out by their ability to be able to produce alternative texts, then in mass, Internet-based societies such creativity is potentially in the hands of literally millions of people. Such a situation has an emancipatory potential that George Orwell could not have foreseen. Of course everywhere activists and critical voices are faced by powerful agents of spin, paid experts and media corporations in an unequal struggle to influence public opinion. But we would do well to remind ourselves of the dramatic reconfiguration of power and opportunities for critical forms of dissent that are currently opening out.

While not wishing to argue that the development of the Internet does not offer considerable possibilities for more active forms of citizenship and creative authorship, I think some of the claims argued thus far are in danger of being overstated. Notably much of the literature on social movements and the Net has very little to say about the state more generally. Here I would want to argue that it is a mistake to neglect the considerable power that the state has in respect of how different social movements are perceived and monitored. Castells, in this respect, has a tendency to suggest that the state has declined in power in respect of its ability to govern communicative relations within society more generally. While he recognises that states maintain a considerable amount of coercive power, this is never central to the analysis. We also need to remember that citizenship, for most of the population most of the time, still remains overwhelmingly national rather than global in orientation. In addition many states through the development of broadcasting systems, regulatory apparatus and of course the prominent position of national forms of politics remain central in the ways that ideas of global civil society are not. These systems of communication are ambivalent creations as they seek to enhance civic forms of citizenship while also maintaining a sense of loyalty amongst the citizenry. On the one hand, organisations such as the BBC are public service providers that hold in check the populism of the market and provide a valuable service to citizens. On the other, however, public service providers are far from 'neutral' and remain orchestrated by the state that is directly involved in the appointment of their ruling bodies and can exert other pressures. Finally we might remind ourselves that television (and especially the more powerful networks) is more central in defining most people's understanding of the political in the way radical websites are not.

We also need to consider the existence of the 'secret state' that is rarely fully under democratic control. E.P. Thompson (1970) remains a significant figure in this respect charting the rise of an increasingly authoritarian, militaristic and repressive state in Britain during the 1970s and 1980s. Here Thompson identifies the rise of an increasingly centralised and regulative political system, the role that the media plays in policing dissent, the erosion of civil liberties, the enlargement of police powers but also an uncivil state. The state is then an ambivalent body, protecting freedom on the one hand while often eroding it on the other.

In more recent times, Zygmunt Bauman (2006) has argued that the social state has been replaced by the security state. In other words, the state is not so much legitimated through the benefits of social citizenship but more as a means to protect an increasingly anxious population from the Other (the poor, vagrants, terrorists, etc.). If the social state aided democracy in that it offered citizens a sense of collective solidarity then the security state feeds off fear (Bauman 2006: 155). But this is not the return of totalitarian power where the state seeks to replace civil society. Instead the civil realm becomes ever more privatised where individuals are increasingly left to their own devices. It is not the fear of the state's totalitarian power that dominates modern democratic life but the fear of unemployment and poverty. Fear under neo-liberalism becomes translated as collective insecurity rather than Orwellian state control. For Bauman (2009) freedom in such a consumer-orientated society becomes a way of travelling light and living flexibly. Yet such a way of living and imagining freedom has disastrous consequences for the idea of community, solidarity and the common good that find their institutional expression in the social state. The other side of individualisation, consumerism and the rise of the security state is the decline of meaningful citizenship. Similarly Ulrich Beck (1998: 3) discusses the rise of what he calls 'freedom's children'. By this he means that freedom for many young people means both a withdrawal from politics and an intense investment in the value of personal freedom, self-development and control over their time. Personal freedom (sometimes in the guise of consumerism) has come to replace public freedom.

If Orwell was concerned that totalitarian power would come to dominate the public and private spheres, Bauman (2000) argues this should no longer be the principle concern of critical thought. Rather than pointing to the way new media has revived public space, Bauman (2000: 40) more accurately observes that 'public space is increasingly empty of public issues'. The task of critical thinking in such a setting is to win back spaces for public discussion and not to defend the private realm from attack by the state. Rather than the privatisation of public issues the public sphere needs to be rebuilt by focusing on questions such as justice, fairness and ideas of freedom beyond consumerism. Freedom here, as with Orwell and Arendt, becomes redefined not as non-interference, but as the possibility of public voice and discussion. If Arendt and Orwell could be forgiven in their own times of being concerned about the totalitarian power of the state, for Bauman our own questions of freedom are more concretely concerned with the withering of public space, insecurity, consumerism and the growth of the security state. Bauman (1988) argues that Orwell's vision of unfreedom as citizens who are too controlled to rebel should now be replaced with an appreciation of the way that consumer freedom masks a society built upon the exploitation of others in a global sweatshop economy, the downgrading of the social state and a prevalent sense of insecurity. These features continue to have totalitarian aspects, but equally we need to appreciate the increasing dominance of a market-driven society unlike that experienced by Arendt or Orwell.

The problem of downgrading the Big Brother model of unfreedom, however, is at least fourfold. First, as I have indicated, states remain powerful actors even within the context of a global market economy and these are central to questions of freedom. If it is true that personal freedom has come to replace public freedom this can be mapped through changes that have been driven by state policy. As we shall see, the development of a mass consumer culture and neo-liberal economics are intimately connected to a politics of the state. Second, the market society or business-driven society is explicitly authoritarian in style and practice. The new economy has arguably put increasing amounts of power in the hands of powerful corporate elites undermining the practice of democracy and the nation state more generally. For instance, the overt promotion of a market-based culture reduces the public spaces available for alternative forms of thought and more experimental forms of practice. Market-driven reforms have not enhanced the power of ordinary people in their workplaces, schools, health care and education or in a number of other institutional settings. Third, we should also remember that it is the state that sets the civic tone and culture of a particular society. In this respect, states can to a greater or lesser extent, through the regulation of public and civic places, education and the development of specific political cultures, emphasise the importance of civic participation, ethnic nationalism, multiculturalism or numerous other alternatives. Fourth, Big Brother as the metaphor for the 'control society' now *requires* citizens to be mobile, flexible, future-orientated, focusing upon the 'now' and the immediate while becoming enterprising. In this respect, the mass media now explicitly promotes an entrepreneurial culture (this is currently being done through popular programmes such as *The Apprentice*) while education is being reshaped along more instrumental lines (this includes the downgrading of the humanities and the more explicit promotion of science, technology and business studies). Indeed, there is a general expectation for the population to value upward mobility and market success above any other ethical or creative commitments. Long gone it seems are the concerns of Raymond Williams or Erich Fromm from previous generations about the possibility of developing a genuinely democratic culture based upon alternative forms of cultural production, critical reflection and radically democratised education and media cultures.

The popular television series *Big Brother* (rather than Orwell's own) offers a case in point where individuals enter into a highly controlled and manipulated environment, all seeking to survive being voted off by their fellow contestants and members of the public. This televised spectacle of unfreedom demonstrates the need felt by many young people to become famous and thereby gain access to a glamorous lifestyle of hyper-consumption. Along with the rise of consumerism has come an increasing amount of attention focused upon the performance of the self and acquisitive individualism rather than the kinds of identity and subjectivity required for a democratic society. *Big Brother* overtly celebrates the manufacture through the media of the lives of relatively minor celebrities whose hard work is usually repaid by being granted a few minutes of fame. This and other talent shows, such as *The X Factor*, *The Apprentice* and *Dragons' Den*, all celebrate the virtues of market success, upward mobility and consumerism above all else. If we live in a society where millions of people simply want to live lives of consumer excess, what happens to more authentic ideas of freedom? Has the control society successfully managed to impose a 'one-dimensional' understanding of what a 'successful life' might mean? This argument can of course be exaggerated, but it remains a matter of concern.

Finally, we should add that nation states across the world continue to promote a selective face to their own citizenry. Even within the context of democratic societies, states use their considerable power to promote favourable images of themselves while engaging in dirty wars, falsely imprisoning people, eroding their civil rights and using increasingly sophisticated means of surveillance. This does not mean that states are by their nature evil, but it does mean they are ambivalent creations both protecting and extending freedoms while simultaneously eroding and destroying them. It seems to me that in this context George Orwell's concerns, albeit in a different context, continue to be our own. While it is true that Orwell was mainly concerned with the state, it is not unreasonable to suggest that had he lived longer he would have come to see the arrival of a deeply manipulative market society that sought to ideologically control the population.

Neo-liberalism and cultural politics of shock and cruelty

Orwell's fear of an illiberal and authoritarian society of control is likely to remain a key cultural touchstone for the foreseeable future. For Orwell politics is less about well-being or happiness than freedom. The warning of *Nineteen Eighty-Four* is of a society where public space has been effectively eliminated. The novel continues to be harrowing not only because of thought control but because of the human cruelty and suffering that is both masked and legitimated through the dominance of the Party. This arguably has more than a passing resemblance to the current 'war on terror' where the idea of bringing democracy and human rights to the world has been used to mask an aggressive politics of empire. As Jonathan Schell (2003: 341) has commented 'every empire in history has concealed coarse self-interest behind a veil of noble ideals'. If capitalism has spread inwards into the identities of modern citizens through consumerism it has also, through the war in Iraq, engaged in 'privatisation by occupation' (Boal et al. 2005). The so-called SUV economy (or crude oil driven economy), US demand for oil and the attempt by Washington to export free-market liberal democracy are all important here. In this setting Naomi Klein's (2007) book *The Shock Doctrine* is one of the most significant of recent times. Klein is a well-known global intellectual whose previous work is connected to the so-called anti-globalisation movement, but who, like Orwell, is probably better described as a global social democrat. Like Orwell, Klein is not an academic, writes in plain language, operates for the most part as a journalist and is concerned with the international politics of her time. However, if Orwell had in mind the rise of a pathological state, Klein's focus is on the interconnection between unregulated, out-of-control capitalism and human rights abuse. Her book seeks to explore the interconnections between 'the power of shock', capitalism and the use of torture (Klein 2007: 8). Klein's argument in a nutshell is that the introduction of neo-liberal market reforms since the first 9/11 in Chile (the violent overthrow of a democratically elected government) also requires an intimidated and frightened population. Torture in this respect becomes as much a tool of the market as it does of the state. Klein (2007: 16) writes that the 'goal of this "softening-up" stage is to provoke a kind of hurricane in the mind: prisoners are so regressed and afraid they can no longer think rationally or protect their interests'.

It is in the context of war and social and cultural catastrophe that the market and the state are able to impose radical free-market reforms, driving the logic of neo-liberalism ever further into the culture. If in the first phase of capitalism economic growth requires the conquering of new territories and imperialism, then a later phase seeks to end 'big government' and privatise welfare and public services. The dominant form of pedagogy in this respect comes from the Chicago school of economics under the direction of Milton Friedman, who trained a global generation of economists influencing policy across South America, Britain and later in Iraq. Klein argues that torture and war are used as a means to silence opposition and intimidate the opponents of neo-liberalism. Klein's book is radical as it insists that a politics of human rights abuse and capitalism are deeply related. The problem is that her argument often sounds as though human rights abuse is driven by economics rather than the politics of the state. Jan Nederveen Pieterse (2004: 26) argues that the 'war on terror' is more ideologically than economically driven. The cultural politics of cruelty and human rights abuse is less a matter of corporations than it is an aggressive state politics. The so-called Bush doctrine ('you are either with us or against us') that lies at the heart of the 'war on terror' is more about the power of the state to impose particular economic regimes irrespective of the rule of law. As Orwell well understood, the politics of cruelty requires the operation of a militarised state, secret services and the intimidation of the population. Raymond Williams (1984) points out in an earlier review of Orwell's great book that the free-market politics of the state is politically contradictory in that it removes the welfare function of the state while increasing military spending, surveillance and other systems of law and order. Such a politics is legitimated by the 'capitalist press' and might be legitimately called '*doublethink*' (Williams 1984: 118). Yet if the emergent neo-liberal Empire has produced a global politics of reduced levels of taxation, war, environmental degradation, privatisation and a state increasingly under pressure to downsize this has not ended with the kinds of control that Orwell feared were possible.

While the United States has been able to use its power to press the policies of neo-liberal reform, militarism and cruelty it still remains a democracy. This point perhaps went missing in some of the critical rhetoric that accompanied the 'war on terror' and the urgent need to point to the way that naked power was being used on a global political stage. As Susan Buck-Morss (2003) argues, the fact that the United States remains democratic means that it remains open to criticism in terms of questions of justice, human rights and other civilised standards. If the United States has done much to harm these principles it does not of course make them useless but potentially offers us resources for immanent forms of critique. The Orwellian nightmare only arrives when democratic language and critique has been cancelled by the growth of totalitarian institutions. Democratic cultures, as we saw, remain indebted to an Enlightenment culture of liberty, human rights, autonomous forms of thinking, responsibility and truthful dialogue.

In the context of the 'war on terror' all of these principles have taken a profound battering. In particular I would highlight what Richard Bernstein (2005) has called the revival of the language of evil in the context of the 'war on terror'. To reduce the 'enemy' to 'evil' blocks any attempts to discuss particular policies and strategies and delivers a form of moral certitude that is profoundly anti-democratic. In the war against evil we are called to abandon 'our' values in order to combat fanatics who have no motives and may strike at any moment. There is now a con-siderable amount of evidence that the dominant media has adopted this language quite uncritically while trying to promote a sanitised view of the wars in Iraq and Afganistan.

Once we begin to use the language of 'evil' this betrays any possibility of negotiation or sense that we may indeed be mistaken. As John Keane (2009) argues, democratic practice remains connected to the idea of humility and should be profoundly suspicious of arrogant forms of power. Democracy works best when citizens are able to make judgements, but do so without certitude. Humility becomes a virtue in any truly demo-cratic culture given the extent to which citizens act with a sense of limits and accept that others will indeed see things differently. The practice of democracy should involve a life of constant criticism and scepticism towards the powerful and influential. This practice is uncomfortable with attempts to centralise power, the control of elites or the cult of power worship. If democracies require leaders (which of course they do) we should ensure that they never become 'Big Brother' figures attracting worship rather than sceptical questioning. During the Blair–Bush years it was the practice of democracy that failed to restrain a form of politics that was both arrogant and dispensed with a culture of critique. Notably in Claire Short's (2004) (member of the British Labour government) account of the build-up to the war in Iraq she outlines in detail how the then Prime Minister Tony Blair progressively abandoned the practice of cabinet government for an increasingly autocratic form of politics.

Here we also need to look at how the 'war on terror' sought to legitimate the use of torture. Tzvetan Todorov (2009) argues that the politics of good versus evil unleashed by the 'war on terror' sought to impose good by force. Part of the force required to save 'democracy' was the use of torture. Notably, in terms of public debates, torture has been legitimated through official sources that tend to cover up its use and then defend it as a practice when they have been caught out. Here Orwellian 'doublethink' is in operation as the use of torture is strenuously denied and then only reluctantly admitted while covering-up its systematic use. As Mehdi Hasan (2010) has argued, where torture is admitted there are usually two strategies. The first is to draw upon the 'ticking bomb' argument (this has also been legitimised through popular culture in television shows such as *Spooks* or *24*) where we have 'no choice' but to use torture to save millions of lives. The other argument admits the use of torture, but points to the 'evil' of terrorists. Both of these arguments are deeply misleading and serve to legitimate the use of torture. Here I would argue that if our superiority over 'terrorists' depends upon our values of democracy, human rights and justice, these are quickly abandoned when faced with an 'enemy'. Guantanamo Bay and the politics of Abu Graib should be enough for us to question whether the image that the democratic West likes to promote to itself is also the one being understood by the rest of the world. Indeed, many of the people subjected to torture may be 'guilty' (although many may not) but this still does not make it right (Todorov 2010b).

Orwell reminds us that if torture demonstrates anything it's the capacity of the state to humiliate and crush the individual. If democratic citizenship depends upon our shared capacity for dissent, torture seeks to smother the human spirit. Further, Orwell (2001a) remains important for demonstrating how democracies regularly denounce the barbarism of their 'enemies', while covering up their own violent practices. The problem being that the 'war on terror' has not been met by human rights and peace, but a vengeful security state seeking to erode civic freedoms. The increased powers of surveillance, stop and search and the offence to 'glorify terrorism' (in the 2006 Terrorism Act) all endanger questions of liberty and free speech.

Freedom and democratic pedagogy

If Orwell's later writing became increasingly troubled with the sense that the value of liberty was being eroded in the context of war, totalitarianism and ideological inflexibility, his writing continues to speak to the importance of defending a critical understanding of ideas of freedom against the authoritarian politics of both Right and Left. By 'freedom' Orwell ultimately meant the virtues of democratic socialism namely liberty and justice. If Orwell is important because he imagined freedom's nightmare, he also sought to write about the antidote to the poison of the Big Brother society. Orwell (2001b) is most explicit about questions of liberty and justice in his work on the mass unemployment of the 1930s. In particular Orwell is keen to point out how the material privileges and liberties of the middle-classes are actually built upon the exploitation of others often hidden away and distant. Orwell commented that in a fossil-fuel economy it is the dirty work and low pay of English coal miners that freedoms are built upon. Orwell understood that this 'opposition' could only be addressed through a passionate socialist politics where working-class people come to value the liberty and freedom to develop themselves. However, the problem that Orwell struggles with is whether it is possible to square the circle between the desire on the part of middle-class intellectuals for liberal freedoms and the need for economic security more keenly felt by the working class. Here Orwell (2001c: 437) asks whether the ordinary people of 'the street ever feel that freedom of the mind is as important and as much in need of being defended as his daily bread?' Orwell understood that this 'opposition' could only be addressed through a progressive democratic politics whereby working-class people come to value the liberty and freedom to develop themselves in a way that is only possible once poverty and economic uncertainty are left behind.

Orwell was critical of middle-class socialists who have little contact with the lives of the urban poor and of Marxist intellectuals who prefer a language of abstraction to more critical forms of public engagement. Ultimately Orwell (1968e: 28) carried this argument through to his own prose claiming that since his experiences in the Spanish civil war he had written 'against totalitarianism and for democratic Socialism'. In the final section of his book on urban poverty, Orwell (2001b) is deeply critical of a technocratic form of socialism that seeks to reduce questions of liberty and justice to the need to utilise technology to expand production. Orwell's socialism cannot be reduced to simply hoping to make people feel 'better off' but implies the complex interaction of the values of liberty and justice. While some of the language that Orwell uses is unnecessarily harsh his overall point is to develop a form of political pedagogy that is able to engage with the concerns of many ordinary working- and middle-class people. Unless they are able to do this Orwell fears many people will become attracted to a fascism that promises a more secure future, less marked by mass unemployment. Unless democratic thought and practice can offer a future beyond mass poverty while upholding certain democratic virtues, then many may become attracted to authoritarian solutions. Here Orwell proposes a form of political pedagogy where critical intellectuals act as 'organic intellectuals' able to dialogue with ordinary people about their problems and concerns (Gramsci 1988: 321). His concern here was that without such an engagement democrats and radicals could easily become dismissed as 'cranks' with little connection to the lives of most people. As Henry Giroux (2006) argues, it is not only that critical intellectuals need to open up new sites of learning and democratic engagement, but that this can only be done if a diversity of experiences are taken into account in this process.

A free society depends on people who are not afraid of freedom. Orwell makes special mention of the education system. Freedom is unlikely to be experienced as a value if the education system is reduced to training for employment, but by engaging with unusual and difficult ideas individuals are offered the possibility of developing a questioning and critical life. Such democratically inspired individuals, Orwell (2001c: 437) hoped, are unlikely to be satisfied with a society that is overly totalitarian or 'organised like a beehive'. Ultimately for Orwell this did not mean a perfect or utopian society but rather one where economic security and liberal freedoms could be preserved while keeping more overtly author-itarian solutions to social problems at bay. The cause of freedom as Orwell saw it was not best served either by an unregulated economy or an authoritarian state but by shared cultures of criticism. Orwell's definition of freedom seeks to connect the socialist and liberal definitions of freedom while offering a critique of totalitarian power. Here Orwell (1968e: 28) was explicitly aware that he wrote to draw attention to injustice, but also because he wished 'to make political writing into an art'. Orwell's concerns were multifarious and yet his democratic spirit in all its ambiguity and complexity remains just as compelling now as it did when he died in London in 1950.

4

CULTURAL FREEDOM

So far the argument has been that the idea of freedom involves the emergence of a society that has liberal institutions, civil rights, the possibility of voice, a social state, relatively secure forms of employment, a diverse media of mass communication and an education system less concerned with training and ideological indoctrination than the development of the capacity to be creative, learn and think. This vision fits with a liberal socialist agenda that developed over the course of the twentieth century. Liberal socialism basically sought to promote a society built upon civic freedoms as well as equality, social solidarity and security. A more emancipated future society would not arrive through revolution, but through the progressive reform of public institutions, the idea that a liberal educated culture was for everyone, and the development of common forms of citizenship that included the welfare state. The liberal socialist tradition has inevitably been reinvented over time but probably finds its best early expression in the work of Hobhouse writing at the beginning of the twentieth century. Hobhouse (1964) explicitly seeks to connect the values of liberty and a more communally orientated collectivism that was finding expression in the working-class movement. Like other liberals Hobhouse was keen to point out that freedom could only be safeguarded through equal treatment before the law. Liberty was not simply doing as you pleased but required civil institutions to regulate behaviour. There is no freedom without constraint. Further, equality and liberty are not always at loggerheads with one another as the working-class movement's desire for the regulation of industry, decent housing and education would actually enhance the liberty of the community. For our purposes, however, what remains significant is the link that Hobhouse discovered between liberty and self-development:

> The foundation of liberty is the idea of growth. Life is learning, but whether in theory or practice what a man genuinely learns is what he absorbs, and what he absorbs depends upon the energy which he himself puts forth in response to his surroundings.
>
> *Hobhouse (1964: 66)*

Like Mill before him, Hobhouse felt that a moral character was not created through conformity, but in learning to direct the self. This offers the possibility of citizens being allowed to learn from their mistakes, to change their minds, and perhaps to fail differently next time. For Hobhouse, it is in pursuing our own good restrained by the rule of law that we also expand the common good. Unlike many liberals of the nineteenth century, what becomes explicit in Hobhouse is the debt that is owed to the community more generally. Individuals are not simply left to fend for themselves but need to be provided with a 'living wage' and a guaranteed minimum beneath which a civilised life clearly would not be possible. Hobhouse contrasted his version of liberal socialism with the 'mechanical socialism' of Marxists and the top down 'official socialism' of technocratic planners. Hobhouse argued that, while the individual had responsibilities to the community, the driving force of liberalism was the liberty to develop ourselves.

As we have seen the idea of freedom was central to the ideas of the New Left that emerged across Europe and North America in the 1960s. The aim here was to radicalise social liberalism and social democracy and democratise society's dominant institutions. The dream of this historical period was to make liberal ideas of freedom meaningful for the many rather than the few. However, since this period freedom has become market freedom. The historian Tony Judt (2010) has argued that after 1945 Western European societies were especially keen to ameliorate the human catastrophe of two world wars and mass unemployment that played a crucial role in the rise of totalitarianism across the continent. The development of stable republics based upon equal rights, democratic governments and social and economic security as we have seen has been progressively replaced by more market-orientated governments. The dream of a progressive liberal and socially just society, where the practice of freedom is more than the desire to make money and for upward mobility, is passing. This of course does not mean that this ground might not be won back, but we have to be clear that the neo-liberal market reforms of the 1980s have had a huge effect on the idea of freedom. But it is not true to say that liberal socialism was simply abandoned during this time.

After the fall of the Berlin Wall in 1989 the game seemed to be up for many on the liberal Left. The collapse of the wall was widely presented to the public as a victory of the capitalist West over the communist East. This particular narrative displaced the role that many liberal socialist societies had played in Western Europe in connecting liberal freedoms with ideas of social solidarity. Yet this narrative had a degree of plausibility given that the Right in Europe and North America, embodied in the leadership of Thatcher and Reagan, had pursued policies that were hostile to organised labour and welfare, that reduced taxation, privatised public utilities and sought to return to more vocationally orientated education. The programmes of the New Right were presented to the public as increasing freedom (enhancing the role of private enterprise and the explicit promotion of consumerism), rolling back the state and heavily investing in the military and the police. In terms of the liberal socialist agenda I am seeking to defend, this period might be better characterised as rolling back freedom. There was a marked growth in social and economic inequality, a progressive curtailment of trade unions and perhaps most pervasive of all the growth of the idea that the point of living was to get rich. This not only helped undermine ideals of public service, but also shredded the post-war idea that high taxation could be justified as it was an investment in the wider good of the community. Social liberalism sought to defend the state not only because it offered people collective security against the perils of unemployment, care in sickness and health, but also the possibility of gaining access to a decent education. Notably during the 1980s the social liberalism that had more or less dominated since the end of the Second World War came increasingly under attack. Rather than the state being involved in the expansion of freedom it was seen as creating both 'dependency' upon its resources, and restricting the freedom of business and enterprise more generally. In Britain and North America many on the political Right began to describe taxation as a form of theft, complaining about the decline of the work ethic (benefit levels being set at too high a level) and that the new freedoms of the 1960s had largely supported a corrupt culture of immorality and moral relativism.

The Right during this period liked to evoke the idea of Victorian values. The idea was that the capitalist culture of the Victorian period was less restricted by the state and that the free market enabled the growth of freedom and self-reliant individuals. Further, that a common morality had become eroded by the 'free thinking' of the 1960s. This had created a generation of young people who did not know how to behave and who needed to be disciplined and controlled. It is for these reasons that the political philosopher John Gray (2007) argues that this period saw the Right (rather than the Left) embracing an inflexible utopian ideology that sought to drive out collectivism. If it was the Left who were the utopians in the 1960s dreaming of a new society based upon educated liberal freedoms for the many, this was replaced by a politics that was far more pragmatic in orientation. During the 1980s it was the political Right who grabbed the dream of freedom and made it their own. The language of markets, prosperity and the dream of a life of wealth without social responsibility remade the political Right during the 1980s. It was then during the 1990s that the Left sought to reinvent itself through the idea of the 'third way'.

Third way liberal socialism

The third way has been dismissed by many on the Left as neo-liberalism in disguise or Thatcherism by other means. Both of these arguments are mistaken. The third way was a concerted attempt on the part of the Left to think through what liberal socialism might mean in new times. Given the intellectual dominance of the Right during the 1980s there was evidently a need for social democracy to reinvent itself. More specifically the golden age of social democracy had seemingly passed not only because of the political dominance of the Right, but due to some significant sociological shifts as well. The key architect of the third way was the eminent sociologist Anthony Giddens.

As a leading sociologist it is not surprising that Giddens locates the need for a rethinking of social democracy in the context of radical social change. These changes include the globalisation of markets and cultural identities, the development of lifestyle diversity, the weakening of the divide between Right and Left in a post-socialist world, the development of new political agencies outside of the conventional theatre of party politics, and the rise of an ecological politics of risk that questions the Left/Right polarity. These features are enough to suggest that if liberal socialist policies are to survive they need to be radically rethought. However, what makes the third way distinctive is the argument that 'politics should take a positive attitude towards globalisation' (Giddens 1998: 64). While recognising that neo-liberal forms of globalisation can indeed have a destructive impact we should beware of retreating into a politics of protectionism. Third way politics not only seeks to break with old-style statist social democracy and neo-liberalism, but also offers a new politics of citizenship that presses 'no rights without responsibilities' (Giddens 1998: 65). By this Giddens is concerned to highlight that old-style social democracy had oftened stressed rights over duties. This argument certainly has a point in relation to a social liberalism where the rights to develop the self are rarely balanced in terms of a discussion of the responsibilities of the citizen. However, as we shall see, there are other currents within this tradition where this criticism is somewhat wide of the mark.

The key question for Giddens in the context of the decline of tradition and the rise of lifestyle politics becomes, what are our obligations in a fast moving and increasingly global world? Giddens argues that in the modern world the central questions are no longer about social justice, but how we should live in the context of the decline of tradition. Due to the development of a knowledge-based and information economy citizens are able to gather a wealth of detail on topics from reports on schools to health-care advice and from details of air travel to 24-hour news; this has led to an increasing questioning of taken-for-granted assumptions by a computer- and media-literate population. Citizens are increasingly making calculations as to what is safe to eat, where to put their savings, what are the best schools and even which religion is right for them.

Despite the development of new political initiatives, risks and opportunities, the state remains central to the third way. However, Giddens argues that we need to radically rethink the relationship between the state and civil society in order to help foster a deeper involvement in the political process by community and local initiatives. Whereas neo-liberals wish to shrink the state, the third way is all about a reconstructed national state. Here the state should engage in processes that seek what Giddens (1998: 72) calls the 'democratising of democracy'. This involves constitutional reform, the expansion of the public sphere, the devolution of power, citizens' juries and more flexible decision structures. These features would increase the capacity of civil society to take a more active role in self-government, breaking from old-style statist social democracy whereby the potential of civil society was rendered largely passive. The new role adopted by the state should build upon democratising pressures to help develop a society of 'responsible risk takers' (Giddens 1998: 100). Such action is needed to redraw debates in respect of equality where renewed emphasis is placed not upon equality of opportunity but the 'redistribution of possibilities' (Giddens 1998: 101).

Third way politics aims to combat the growth of two kinds of exclusion to be found where both elites and an underclass begin to live their lives cut off from mainstream society. In this respect, exclusion at the top and bottom of society becomes a major problem in advanced industrial societies that are witnessing rapid growth in income inequality. The way these groups are encouraged to maintain a shared commitment to the community is through the maintenance of social solidarity through institutions that promote a good quality public education, sustain health resources and genuine public amenities that aim to provide an inclusive compact amongst diverse social groups. As Giddens (1998: 108) argues 'only a welfare system that benefits most of the population will generate a common morality of citizenship'.

The third way seeks to couple the practice of responding 'positively' to technological change and global markets with a renewed emphasis upon obligations in an attempt to remodel an inclusive society. The reform of the public sector is essential to prevent the relatively well off from contracting out of goods and services (they need to be offered expanded forms of choice) and thereby increasingly cutting themselves off from the poor. These features have particular implications for a politics of education, the case for high-quality forms of education being a necessity for everyone in the context of increased global competition. Further, as we have already seen, third way arguments make a great deal of the capacity of citizens to make 'informed' choices in the context of the free availability of information.

But many have claimed that the third way had too little to offer the poor other than market discipline and that it is mainly concerned to stop the middle classes from opting out of public institutions. The third way information economy arguments inspired by Giddens do not offer enough reflection on questions of inequality and the radical curtailment of the freedom of those who do not have the educational ability to be able to make use of new sources of information. If the idea of a post-traditional society is overstated at least the third way recognises some of the challenges that any liberal socialist government would need to face in an information age. All governments are today confronted by sceptical publics who are used to information technology and concerned about value for money. However, the third way arguments generally fail to recognise that this is mostly restricted to middle-class publics.

If the third way contributed more on questions of responsibility than freedom it ultimately failed to promote a more responsible society. The market crash of 2008 demonstrated that third way arguments had failed to be adequately attentive to the need to regulate and control the market. The increasing divide between rich and poor, progressive use of the logic of the market in public sector reforms and the development of an irresponsible consumerism all gathered pace during this period. The third way could and should have done more to learn from its own liberal socialist past. Historically this has meant support for an interventionist state that sought to contain the market, address inequality and protect civil rights. R.H. Tawney (1961) argued that capitalist society in this respect seeks to emphasise rights as opposed to responsibilities. This ultimately leads to a destructive form of individualism that simply ends with rights to secure for oneself a privileged education and high levels of personal consumption. By reconnecting rights and responsibilities, Tawney sought to emphasise a sense of obligation to the wider community. Such a move, as we shall see, opens the possibility of citizens not only being offered relatively equal opportunities, but also an educated culture that enables them to develop themselves as cultural beings, not simply as raw material for 'use' in the workplace. In other words, the relatively privileged are charged with the responsibility to make sure other members of the community enjoy similar freedoms to develop the self that they have enjoyed.

The demand that ordinary working-class people have a right to an intellectual life and that the education system should prepare its citizens for a life within a shared community has a long history within liberal socialist thinking. The historian Jonathan Rose (2001) demonstrates how within the working-class during the twentieth century, before the rise of the mass media, there existed a culture of mutual improvement based less upon reading radical texts, more upon complex works of literature. What I continue to find valuable about the liberal socialist tradition is the idea that personal freedom should not be reduced to the needs of the economy and its suspicion of authoritarianism of all kinds. As Tawney (1964) argued, the liberal socialist critique of capitalism was as concerned with questions of inequality and poverty as it was with the possibility of developing a new politics of citizenship. This new politics was concerned about the effects of atomised individualism and sought to connect rights, community and responsibility. He recognised that economic power could undermine democracy and the quality of civic life by converting education into a means of training for the economy. Tawney (1964: 168) argued that liberal socialists were concerned that 'to lead a life worthy of human beings is confined to a minority, what is commonly called freedom would more properly be described as privilege'. For Tawney, a community that made life worth living would need to be built upon a sense of mutual responsibility and the freedom to develop the self. It is in terms of questions of cultural freedom, especially in relation to education, that the third way is lacking. Here, despite the third way's attempts to improve the 'level' of educational attainment, it has too little to say about the quality of education more generally. Too often third way arguments leave the quality of education to be determined by league tables, standardised tests and other technocratic features that seem to suggest that education was simply a passport for success in the wider economy. This is a great shame as the liberal socialist tradition has much to contribute on questions of cultural freedom.

Educated liberal socialism

Many liberal socialists, such as John Dewey in America and George Orwell and R.H. Tawney in Britain, were explicitly concerned with the reform of the education system. This, they felt, should not teach vocational skills or be built upon rote learning, but was the place where young people would learn to be free. This was done by students engaging in complex literature, working on their own problems and engaging with different cultural traditions while being mixed in with other members of the community. Freedom needed to become a daily practice if it was to take root in the context of everyday life. Education should be connected to the explicit aim of getting students to appreciate the value of thinking for themselves, not simply learning to pass exams. It was arguments of this kind that led to the setting up of comprehensive forms of education and genuinely public schools. The education of the young was a matter of public concern and responsibility and could not be left to the market. Here there was an explicit concern to think of young people as citizens in the making who were not simply 'blank slates' to be written over by teachers and educationalists. Unfortunately these ideas never really went far enough, with many state-run schools being of poor quality while remaining training grounds for the wider economy. However, the desire to remake education along these grounds was particularly keenly felt amongst the most responsible sections of the labour movement. Rather than simply concerning themselves with the not unimportant question of wage levels many in the trade union movement also sought to gain access to a broader education for the vast majority of ordinary people. For Richard Hoggart (1957), the development of the 'affluent society' pressed the desire for consumer goods over the need to educate the self. Hoggart feared that what he called the spirit of 'democratic egalitarianism' helped foster scepticism around claims that some cultures and ways of life are better than others. If what counts is not how well read or educated you are then there is nothing to prevent the principle aim of life becoming how to make as much money as quickly as possible. Indeed, Hoggart feared that with the development of new cultural and leisure industries many would simply give up on the need to 'better the self' and instead 'comfort the self'. While many have dismissed this attitude as snobbish, what this criticism misses is the way it can be said to be historically connected to the more normative aims of the working-class movement.

The labour movement during the nineteenth century was concerned that an unregulated capitalist economy would lead to an increasingly unequal society, thereby undermining a sense of community and solidarity. The market relied on a world of selfish competition where making money was valued over the need to provide welfare, participate in the civic life of the community and expand education. This period is probably best captured by Robert Tressell's (2005) classic novel *The Ragged Trousered Philanthropists*. Written during the early part of the twentieth century the novel describes the social and cultural condition of a group of working-class painters and decorators as they struggle to survive in a harsh and cruel world. The novel has become a classic not only because it tells a good story, but for the often humorous ways it describes a condition of unfreedom and the struggle to survive. The workers are ruthlessly exploited by their employers and denied basic levels of welfare, suffer abject poverty and daily forms of disrespect and humiliation, fear unemployment and are denied the possibility of being able to think for themselves. One of the most striking aspects of the novel are the scenes where workers are struggling to understand an oppressive system given that many have only received the most basic education and the newspapers they read support the interests of the employers. Perhaps not surprisingly this novel is now considered a classic of working-class fiction and has been handed down by generations of working people as the text that explains the workings and oppressions commonly associated with a market-driven society. While the novel makes plain somewhat didactically that the workers have interests in a different economic system the real force of the narrative emerges through its ability to reveal that currently liberal ideals are for the many (if not for the few) a sham.

But it was due to arguments like this, as I have indicated, that liberalism took a social turn in the twentieth century. After the rise of fascism and communism, the mass unemployment of the 1930s and two world wars, European societies sought to construct a new economic order. This was a world built upon the legal recognition of trade unions, full employment and prosperity, rising levels of education, a liberal media culture and of course a decent education for everyone. This was a vision that drew together Western Europe and North America and led to a period of genuinely inclusive citizenship built upon the attempt to uphold equal civil, political and social rights. Of course, this was not the arrival of a utopian society, but it was the aim of many through the state to develop a genuinely inclusive and civilised society. These societies still contained exploitation, unemployment and inequality, but offered a sense of rising expectation for many ordinary people.

It was not until the 1960s, however, that feminism and black politics started to ask questions about the ways in which women and ethnic minorities more generally had been relegated to the condition of second-class citizenship. As the possibility of an educated and more inclusive society was being created for many people during this period it is not surprising that this was a time of aspiration and optimism. Indeed, if the working-class fiction of the early part of the twentieth century depicted a prison-house world of exploitation, then the working-class novels of the 1960s are often ambivalent tales of upward mobility. Here, if moving class background was problematic given the implications it had for cultural identity, there was at least an accompanying sense of possibility as well. Stan Barstow's (1964) classic novel of this period, *A Kind of Loving*, tells a story of male working-class aspiration and upward mobility. While the narrative rests mainly upon the protagonist Victor Brown's troubled relationship with his girlfriend, Ingrid, the novel creates a sense of the broadening of horizons experienced by many working-class people seeking to improve the quality of their lives through consumption or education. Many of Victor Brown's siblings are able to enjoy employment opportunities their parents could only dream of and purchase homes of their own, labour-saving devices, new consumer items like television sets and other aspects we commonly associate with the new consumer society. While it is true the novel is mainly concerned with male occupational mobility and the desire to avoid the perceived entrapment of marriage, 'freedom' is not conceived merely in monetary terms. Victor Brown is keen to explore the world of classical music, which to previous generations of his family would be out of reach as well as regular trips to the cinema and the theatre. As with Robert Tressell, there is a sense that 'improving the self' is bound up with 'educating the self'. To improve the self is to become better than we were previously.

This has a deep link to questions of freedom. The meaning of 'improving the self' contained within these novels from different times is the ability to think for yourself and to explore other vocabularies outside of those within which you are currently located. For the working-class people of Tressell's and Barstow's novels, to become educated is not simply a matter of becoming middle class as, in a class-divided society, this is understood not surprisingly as a source of considerable ambivalence. Education is not simply seen as a means of gaining access to more and better employment. Instead, it is the role of education not only to raise critical questions about the host culture, but to make possible other ways of seeing. Freedom in this setting can't be reduced to a question of having more options or choices, but instead opens the possibility of new ways of being that you are free to explore. The optimism that can be detected in this and other working-class novels of the 1960s is a sense not only of the personal freedoms that might be associated with affluence, but also of quite literally other possibilities as well. A world that had seemed to be tightly scripted and restricted is suddenly open to new horizons and different kinds of experience. These novels seem to suggest that if you are poorly educated then even if you become 'better off' materially your ability to live a life of freedom is hampered. To return to some of the themes of the previous chapter, unless we have the ability to form a critical understanding of the world we are likely to become prey to ideological strategies, simplistic forms of understanding and an inability to think. It is this concern that best ties together personal and public forms of freedom. The task of becoming free is poorly located exclusively in personal or public life, but crucially concerns the capacity to engage with the voice of others at a number of different levels. These novels are significant as they capture the basic liberal socialist idea that the freedom we experience can be related to the value that is placed upon education for the whole community.

My argument here is that cultural freedom is not simply a question of speaking in your own voice or simply having the right to shock, but is more explicitly concerned with what the radical educationalist Henry Giroux (1993) calls border crossing. The aim is to enable learners to negotiate complex languages of alternative narratives and experiences that permanently displace ideas of the centre and the margin. As Giroux (1993: 369) writes:

> literacy as an emancipatory practice requires people to read, speak, and listen to the language of difference, a language in which memory becomes multiaccentual and dispersed, and resists permanent closure.

This is a language that offers learners the possibility of negotiating borders and understanding complex forms of cultural difference. Cultural borders may be explored through explorations in music, history, art, philosophy or in more scientific writing. This is clearly a demanding task that would find most educators falling short. However, the idea of education enabling students to make sense of such complex cultural borders as class, gender, race, religion or sexuality is very important if they are to learn new vocabularies and avoid being fixed into place by more normalising aspects of our culture. For example, Raymond Williams's (1962) novel *Border Country* (another great working-class novel) opens up a complex language involving the crossing of cultural as well as temporal and spatial borders. Centrally the novel maps a number of borders concerned with the country and the city, class background, public and private as well as past and present. Williams's own life was centrally concerned with borders and an appreciation of their political and personal significance. Here my argument is that a democratic and culturally inclusive education will inevitably be involved in complex processes that invite students to reinterpret and rethink complex borders in terms of their own reading and experiences. Education becomes valued precisely because when it is properly practised it is concerned with the development of the self and the crossing of intellectual and multicultural borders. To become educated is to have access to a broad range of vocabularies through which to understand the wider society.

X Factor education

If the formal education system is one place of learning then the media is another. The rapid undermining of a culture of public service television has allowed the gradual rise of more commercial forms of broadcasting. If we add to this picture the development of computer games, popular reality television and new communications technologies we could easily argue that it is now market-based media that is a much more powerful educator than the education system. The culture of branding, corporations, logos and celebrity is now pervasive in democratic societies. Undoubtedly much of the material produced by commercial corporations is both entertaining and fun; however, there are considerable dangers if the young are converted into indifferent consumers. The power of large corporations such as Disney to shape the horizons and passions of the young is radically underestimated by many liberals. Of course there are equal dangers in parents simply banning commercial culture from the home. What is required is the development of more critical forms of understanding and engagement on a range of questions that are unlikely to be problematised by much mainstream culture. While many critical programmes are still made in the public service tradition the cost of indifferent consumerism needs to be raised within education. Here the key question critical educators are compelled to ask is not only what are our freedoms, but also what our responsibilities should be in the face of inequality and injustice, ecological devastation and increasingly diverse societies. These issues can't be readily answered simply by returning to earlier phases of liberal socialism, but require us to ask new questions in new times. Here the young require a deep knowledge of past traditions and events that helped shape the present. The dangers and unfreedoms that were faced by our ancestors should help in the quest for a more engaged citizenry. But this is unlikely to have much effect if education is simply seen as a passport to market success. Much of today's commercial culture values the capacity to achieve instant success, immediate wealth or fame. The moral indifference of many contemporary citizens has been reproduced by a culture of hyper-consumption and political indifference. It is this feature that I call 'X *Factor* education'. It is primarily a market culture that closes the eyes of many citizens to other ethical possibilities as to how we should live our lives. As the philosopher Paul Ricoeur (2007) argues we are all charged with the question of how we should live in a shared global context of injustice. How do we pursue questions of justice or freedom without them being turned into forms of hatred and retaliation? Indeed, justice without compassion usually ends in cruel forms of indifference or, even worse, vengeance. The freedom to pursue these questions necessarily requires a sense of responsibility to others no matter how much we feel we have been wronged. These are inevitably complex questions that not only ask us to rethink the priorities of the cultural traditions within which we find ourselves located, but also the civic indifference that has more often been fostered by the dominant market culture. Indeed, as we shall see, these questions have recently taken on a renewed importance on the international stage.

5

COSMOPOLITAN FREEDOM

The struggle for freedom so far in our story has been largely internal to nation states. The state is an ambivalent site as without it we have no freedom (or security for that matter) but it also continually threatens the civic order. The good society is dependent upon a number of civil rights without which freedom would soon disappear. The freedom to think, debate, argue, create, organise ourselves politically, gain protection of the law and not to suffer unnecessary bodily hardship all depend upon the state. However, as we have seen, states may decide to turn their backs on the poor, convert our education into vocational training, commericalise our culture and of course deny our basic civil rights. What is most troubling of all is that this can all be done in the name of freedom. It is because of freedom that we need to slash welfare benefits, close down intellectual debates, turn our media over to large conglomerates and restrict the rights of citizens. This is indeed happening today in a world where market freedom is increasingly coming to define what we take to be liberal freedom. However, as I have been trying to argue throughout, the game is not yet up for more socially liberal under-standings of what we mean by freedom. Freedom is indeed an elastic term that can be given numerous definitions, but it remains a contested idea with a long historical lineage. And how we understand our freedoms is more important than ever.

After the end of the Second World War and the tragedy of the Holocaust, the idea that humans required minimal guarantees in respect of freedom gathered pace. This was not an attempt to create a more homogenous world, but there was a desire to establish a human bond that could advance and protect the rights of vulnerable human beings. The experience of totalitarian Europe and the arrival of murderous regimes that dispensed with liberal human freedoms were crucial in the development of a new form of global politics that sought to put aside national interests. Richard Falk (2000), reflecting on more than half a century since the landmark adoption of the 1948 Universal Declaration of Human Rights, is able to argue that human rights is part of an ambivalent success story. Yes of course the world takes seriously some people's rights rather than others, but we should recognise that people the world over have begun to stand up and proclaim their human rights. Similarly Noberto Bobbio (1996) argues that the point is no longer to try philosophically to justify human rights, but how to make them a political reality. The universal freedom of humanity is of course far from a reality, but it remains an ideal to be pursued. We perhaps need to recognise that, if in the 1960s the future seemed to herald a new world being built on human rights and humane development, this has not emerged. As we have seen this was a time when many looked to the future as being marked by the progressive cause of freedom. The development of the so-called Washington Consensus (the global attack on the social state, trade unions and enhancement of the market) has meant that the state has gradually been transformed by the market. The arrival of the market-driven society has seen the transfer of power out of the hands of ordinary voters. This of course provides the context in which many citizens in the USA and across Europe are now voting for aggressive free-market political parties seeking to expand the circle of neo-liberalism. After the disastrous war in Iraq the world has entered a new phase where many are talking less of a global superpower and more of a multi-polar world. The United States remains the globe's most powerful military power, but there are now many regional centres of power from China to Russia and from Brazil to India. Not all of these centres are champions of democracy and human rights (and indeed many use these ideals as a cover for other practices) and the cause of a global consensus on these questions seems as far off as ever.

In light of these developments, might we be better served in describing ourselves as global citizens? There is no meaningful global citizenship without a world state, which in turn is likely to remain a fiction in a world where the most powerful nation states are unlikely to be corrected through the use of international law. A citizen is someone who belongs to a meaningful political community that is governed by the rule of law and who has rights and responsibilities similar to others in that community. On this reading, citizenship remains overwhelmingly although not exclusively located at the level of the nation state. There is of course the struggle for human rights but these are mostly attempts to influence local conditions. Elsewhere some environmental activists have tried to take on the mantle of the global citizen by adopting low-carbon lifestyles. This, they argue, is about taking global responsibility as it is the lives of the poor of the planet which are most likely to be affected by climate change. We should also not forget that there is still the possibility of global compassion and of ordinary citizens responding to appeals for charity beyond the borders of the nation. Here there is an attempt in the era of global media to link local struggles to more global concerns. Protestors against weapons systems, the growth of local food, action taken against the pollution of the seas or the depletion of species diversity are all attempts to link local struggles to more global frameworks. Indeed Anthony Giddens (1992) has pointed out that the questions posed by these movements are not easily translated into the demand for freedom, but are more explicitly concerned with how we might live responsibly in a global age. These are of course important developments but are clearly no substitute for concerted action on the part of states. For example, some of the most vulnerable people in our world today are stateless people or failed asylum seekers who have few if any rights of citizenship. These vulnerable people are often shunted between states, occasionally returned 'home' and sometimes left to perish. Here my point is that the cause of human rights is both noble and just but requires incorporation into citizenship rights.

Despite talk of the global bond of human rights the freedom of citizens mostly depends upon the action of local states. For the time being international law (as we saw in the build-up to the war in Iraq) is comparatively weak when faced with powerful nation states. We might also say the same thing about the development of a global civil society that aims to develop a global consciousness on global questions. In a world where force remains the property of powerful states, then peace is the most likely outcome of a balance between opposing forces. If this seems unnecessarily harsh it is just that a world where our human rights are equally respected is a long way from where we currently stand. Indeed, in the unlikely event of such a world ever emerging it will largely be because states see it as in their interests to support it. This can come about in two main ways. First, nation states can enter into multilateral agreements with one another to promote the cause of human rights and democracy, and second, citizens of these states could demand that the host state lives up to the common language of citizenship. Nation states, as we have seen, will use all the cultural power at their disposal to per-suade citizens that their actions are right as well as just. Here we require an active civil society strongly motivated to hold states in check and to internally promote ideas of human rights and democracy. Of course, much of the discussion in this respect can be global in the media and information age. In our shrunken globe human rights assaults in China, elections in America or media clampdown in Russia become matters of common concern. These features all have effects beyond the borders of particular nation states in our interdependent times. But what matters more than attempts to build a global framework of rules to constrain powerful nation states (I genuinely fear this is doomed to failure) is that critical intellectuals and activists take a 'special' interest in the actions of their host nation on the world stage. As citizens of particular nation states we have a responsibility to point to human rights abuses, injustice and gross insensitivity of our host state whether acting at home or abroad. This is largely because as citizens we are not only responsible for the practices of our own state through the ties of citizenship, but are also best able to influence its development. This of course does not prevent us protesting against or seeking to put pressure on other states; it is just that, despite global flows and developments, politics is likely to remain closer to home than many seem currently to think.

Does this mean that there are no cosmopolitan freedoms? Of course not. It is just that how we understand cosmopolitanism is likely to be heavily influenced by the histories of our own state and development of world regional identity. The problem more often with the talk of global citizenship is that it offers a view from nowhere. By this I mean that some of the philosophers who have proposed this notion have radically underestimated the extent to which ideas of belonging and identity are connected to citizenship and produced for most people in relation to particular places and locations. There are perhaps two main reasons why many intellectuals have been attracted to global citizenship or cosmopolitanism more recently. The first is that the development of a global economy has transferred power upwards out of the hands of states and thereby diminished the practice of citizenship. Here the fear is that states are competing against one another to offer favourable conditions to business and produce a 'race to the bottom', undermining social rights and welfare provision. The second is that the histories of nationalist identification are also the history of exclusivity and barbarism. Rather than citizens with exclusively national passions and interests it is reasoned it is better to have citizens who can think from the point of view of global humanity. The concern for human rights in this setting moves the conversation beyond the nation, but at the same time talks the language of common freedoms. Again these are all worthy aims, but they fail to connect with the ways in which political sentiment, traditions and identities are organised for the vast majority of people. It is not that the idea of human rights might not act as a critical court of appeal in respect of local conditions, but that this is different from arguing that more cosmopolitan forms of imagination could ever replace thicker, more local ties. As Craig Calhoun (2007) notes, the idea of the progressive world citizen as opposed to the regressive nationalist simply invites mystification. The story of the twentieth century, in part stretching across North America and Europe, can be seen as the battle for the recognition of equal rights to national forms of citizenship. Ethnic minorities, women and of course working-class populations have all demanded equal recognition by their host national societies. National forms of citizenship should not simply be seen as backward. Here we are invited to think of the ways in which cosmopolitan and national freedoms might work with rather than against one another.

The problem perhaps emerges when national sentiment is simply opposed to cosmopolitanism. As George Orwell (1968f: 412) noted, if nationalists mainly think in terms of 'competitive prestige' this will inevitably lead to a certain blindness on questions of human rights. This often means condemning the human rights abuses of our 'enemies' while turning a blind eye to those of our own or our 'friends'. However, Orwell also recognises that those who seek to repudiate any sense of nationalism often end up submitting to a greater power (in the case of pacifism) or uncritically supporting another powerful organisation. Orwell (1968f: 418) called this 'transferred nationalism'. In his time Orwell argued that many Marxist intellectuals simply repudiated the idea of their own nation to support the policies of the Soviet Union as it was furthering the cause of socialism. In our time Orwell would undoubtedly have criticised various kinds of religious fundamentalism. How might we think our way out of simply cheering for 'our' home side or uncritically supporting other more powerful movements and organisations? Orwell's answer was intellectual honesty: to admit our feelings of attachment, but to be unafraid to submit them to criticism in terms of more humane standards. This seems to me at least to be about right. Indeed, in the emergent power politics of the time Orwell (1968g) looked to Europe rather than the United States or the Soviet Union as the place where a more *humane* order might emerge. This hope, as we shall see, has been followed by many after him.

Cosmopolitan freedom

The one part of the world where a cosmopolitan polity has come into existence is Europe. After the 1950 European Convention of Human Rights it was able to operate a genuine system of international law that governed European states. The idea of Europe then is not a state, but rather a transnational means of regulating relations between states. This is not, however, a model for the rest of the world, but has grown out of local conditions to address specifically local problems. A genuinely European citizenship can be said to have developed that allows for democratic elections, the formation of common laws and free mobility over national borders for national citizens within Europe. Here we might reasonably begin to talk of a transnational citizenship that does not seek to replace national citizenship. There has been a considerable amount of discussion amongst European intellectuals as to what European citizenship might come to mean. Many such as Ulrich Beck (2006) and Tzvetan

Todorov (2010a) argue that it is Europe's internal sense of cultural difference and lack of cultural homogeneity that promotes a sense of internal critique and debate. It is a sense of Europe's own internal cultural pluralism that promotes awareness of particularity and a suggestion that we might learn to do things differently. This internal cosmopolitan reality means that Europe needs to recognise that it does not have a settled identity, but should instead promote a democratic culture of exchange and debate. Such an idea of Europe would need to break with any concept of being based upon a definite civilisation, substituting inter-mixing and dialogue across cultural borders. If, as I suggested in Chapter 4, the idea of learning can be associated with border crossing and the expansion of our vocabularies, then the same might be said of European citizenship.

Paul Ricoeur (1996) argues that how we transfer memories in the European setting is not a matter of mere instruction. If the stories we tell one another about the past articulate a narrative identity, then we need to develop an appreciation of how the same stories can be worked into different narratives. If we are literally to displace the nation, then this means taking account of other stories. A new European ethos requires the possibility of revising and retelling collective stories that have become rigid and set in stone. The educated intellectual effort to produce plural narratives not only expands our personal and collective repertoires, but also facilitates the ability to dialogue across and in between cultures. As Ricoeur (1996: 8) writes:

> In this exchanging of memories it is a matter not only of subjecting the founding events of both cultures to a crossed reading, but of helping one another set free that part of life and of renewal which is found captive in rigid, embalmed and dead traditions.

Such a process requires not only critical forms of subjectivity but 'narrative hospitality' (Ricoeur, 1996: 8). In this tradition (the active memory of the past) is asked to find a permanent partnership with innovation through reinterpretation. For Ricoeur, the past can be said to have plural futures which may or may not find fruition. In particular it is the central or 'founding' events of historical memory that need to be continually subjected to scrutiny and critical forms of investigation.

If the history of Europe is one of the suffering of war, then the ability to be able to subject national histories to crossed readings while making space for the memory of the Other is an act of hospitality. In Ricoeur's terms forgiveness is not an empty gesture and should not be confused with forgetting. Indeed the recognition of more complex narratives is not only the work of education, but gives up on the desire for revenge in place of deeper forms of cultural exchange. This would require much more than an idea of European history as the eventual triumph of the universal rules of democratic citizenship, but requires that we learn to cross and reinterpret borders. The idea of freedom in this cultural setting is not only about choosing between alternatives, but rather about having the ability to explore different readings and ways of making meaning. If freedom is simply reduced to choice, then some of the complexity of these questions becomes misplaced. European citizenship is not only about the idea of plurality, but perhaps more significantly has come out of a political space created by forgiveness. Europeans for the most part have given up on ideas of vengeance and have instead created common institutions that enable them to construct a common future that constrains the nationalist violence of the past.

However, before we run too far with this idea we need to remember that currently across Europe a number of right wing anti-immigrant political parties are in the ascendancy. If cosmopolitan Europe is to become more than a pleasing self-image it needs to do much more to develop a civic sphere built on inclusive dialogue rather than victimhood. Indeed, from Europe's own past the destructive politics of the 1930s and a wider sense of national resentment ultimately led to the abandonment of democracy. Here the idea of victimhood encourages 'us' to focus on 'our' suffering at the expense of a sense of hospitality towards the Other. Jurgen Habermas (2001) recognises the necessity of European institution-building in the face of common problems, the need to develop an inclusive cosmopolitan identity and the necessity of tackling downward pressure on common systems of welfare. The key question here is whether Europe can develop a sense of cosmopolitan consciousness amongst ordinary citizens. It is only in this setting that European citizenship will become meaningful, replacing European indifference or hostility. Here civic solidarity would be not only a matter for nation states but for Europe as well. The idea of Europe occupies the grounds of utopian institution-building, potentially ushering in an emancipatory post-national citizenship. The problem being of course that such an 'ideal' is a long way from where we currently stand, if it is not entirely unfeasible.

There has also been a considerable amount of public debate about whether Europe can constitute an alternative kind of public space to that represented by the United States. Many public intellectuals have begun to suggest that, given Europe's own internal emphasis on democracy and human rights, it potentially offers a different kind of global power to that of the United States. In the wake of American-led wars in Iraq and Afghanistan, the setting up of Guantanamo Bay and the abuses of Abu Graib the issue was whether Europeans offered a different kind of public politics. Leading European intellectuals Habermas and Derrida (2003) argued that the mass demonstrations of 15 February 2003 against the build-up to the war in Iraq marked the possible emergence of a European public sphere. This helped build a contrast between a Europe built on conciliation and agreement that could be counter-posed to the more aggressive politics of the United States. The problem with this stark contrast, however, is that it obscures Europe's continual reliance upon American military firepower and the extent to which many European governments became complicit with human rights abuses that has stemmed from the 'war on terror'. Similarly Jeremy Rifkin (2004) sought to contrast the failing American dream of competitive, cut-throat capitalism to a European dream based upon social rights, quality of life and a social state. Obviously there is something to this contrast, but the problem is that it considerably underestimates the extent to which neo-liberalism is currently eating into European societies. Perhaps if Europe is being Americanised it is less through the viewing of Hollywood films and eating burgers, and more through the progressive undermining of a citizenship built upon social solidarity. We can still say this while recognising that the so-called European social model is far from homogenous. But we do need to recognise the changing dynamics of global power and not fall too much into the habit of pitting Europe against the United States. As Anthony Giddens (2007) argues, Europe's share of global production is falling, it has an ageing population and many new jobs depend upon the expansion of the knowledge economy more generally. If European welfare depends upon European prosperity then member states will need to be innovative to survive in an increasingly competitive global economy.

This much is beyond doubt; however, the fear remains that without common social policies Europe will be unable to resist the need to both instrumentalise knowledge and push down wage levels in order to compete globally. We do need to remember, however, that the European Union contains a high degree of social and cultural variety, from the relatively egalitarian and strong welfare states of the Scandinavian countries to some of the small-state, low-taxation countries located in Eastern Europe. Indeed Perry Anderson (2009) and Pierre Bourdieu (2003) argue that many intellectuals fail to grasp the reality that Europe is more responsive to business elites than it is to democratic pressures from below. If the European Union began as a way of soldering together human rights, democracy and prosperity it might today more accurately be said to resemble a neo-liberal model. This is the Europe of a central bank and bureaucracy that allows for little in the way of democratic accountability. By expanding EU membership into Eastern Europe it has allowed European capital access to the low-wage economies of the East. Here we find the erasure of the difference between so called free-market America as opposed to a social Europe. If Europe has failed to stand up to the United States in respect of the 'war on terror' the same might be said in respect of the evolution of the low-wage economy. Before we become too pessimistic, however, despite its shortcomings Europe remains a cosmopolitan experiment that has mostly successfully combined peace, human rights and the need for security. That the European project has successfully restrained the aggressive nationalisms of the past remains a remarkable achievement.

Politics and the spectacle

Europe and America might also be said to have shared rather opposed cultures of progressive liberalism. These overlapping traditions expressed themselves in the United States with the New Deal and in Europe with the development of the welfare state. These developments sought to establish civilised standards of well-being for common people. Elites in North America and Europe gave up the politics of the 1930s to defend their privileges at all costs. The aim here was to purposively construct political communities not out of negative freedom, but inclusive ideas of citizenship. As Norman Birnbaum (2001) argues, the period 1945 to 1980 helped construct in Europe and the United States institutions built upon national solidarity. If the achievements of these periods are threatened by neo-liberalism, then so is the ideal of political participation more generally. The social liberalism of the previous era has been defeated not only by neo-liberalism but by a concerted politics of the spectacle. This is the development of a world where the media has gained power in terms of its ability to shape public opinion. The media has become the main battleground rather than trade unions, public meetings or any other face-to-face association that influences public decision making. The overwhelming effect has been to concentrate the minds of ordinary citizens on questions of image rather than substance and to reduce politics to sound bites and questions of strategy. This is less the age of cosmopolitan concern than it is of character assassination, the invasion of privacy and of political questions becoming converted into the eye-catching logic of celebrity. During this period across North America and Europe the practice of newspaper reading has gone into decline and it is now television that dominates the political process. This has the effect of political organisations increasingly organising their campaigns and policies around the rhythms of television. As the cultural critic Richard Hoggart (1970: 151) noted in the early days of mass television, if the medium has the advantage of making knowledge instantaneously available then 'it is a creature of daily or weekly fresh starts'. What matters in terms of the media of mass communication is that the information is 'up to date' and that it has an impact upon audiences immediately. As many commentators have noted, our 'nowist' life shifts attention rapidly from one subject to the next and soon loses any historical reference points. It is not that historical narratives are not present on television but they are fragmented and all competing for attention and network ratings. What becomes obscured is how our ideas of freedom have changed so quickly. The televised spectacle of competing political discourses seeking to make an impact with voters quickly relegates yesterday's news from our minds. It may be that television is able to shift images and perspectives through time and space at a rapid rate, but we are in the process of forgetting who we once were and of recovering less socially generous visions of the future. If a more expansive version of freedom is only possible in situations of narrative hospitality, then is this actually possible in a speed-driven media age? It is perhaps not surprising that a more inclusive social liberalism has found it hard to survive in the consumerist age. Progressive politics depends upon our ability to be able to stand shoulder to shoulder while never sacrificing democratic criticism for solidarity. However, the world today is driven more by greed, profit and inequality than democratic virtues. How then can a more substantive version of freedom hope to survive in our inevitably less-than-perfect world?

6

FREEDOM AND VIRTUE

The main idea of this short book has been to introduce the idea of freedom as historically produced and contested. Ideas of freedom have become centrally important during certain historical periods rather than others. In my account I have suggested that we look carefully at debates within Ancient Greece, the European Enlightenment, the Cold War and what is sometimes called the radical 1960s, though there are of course other periods when ideas of freedom have been intensely debated, such as the Victorian era or during the Russian revolution. We have also seen the rise of neo-liberal thinking, which has radically altered our common understandings of freedom. In a sense the historical thrust of the debate has been to argue, against Marxism and liberal ideas of negative liberty, that more convincing as well as more feasible ideas of freedom can be found in the tradition of social liberalism. This tradition, as we have seen, has mainly emerged out of American and European traditions of thinking but is not their exclusive property. The basis of this idea is that a free society needs to draw upon the values of liberty as well as social solidarity. Freedom here is both a public and private virtue. That we are able to lead the lives of our choosing without being overwhelmed by the anxiety of losing our employment, while having access to adequate resources, a state that can care for us and an education and public sphere that can stimulate our intelligence have all been central features in the argument. As we saw these concerns stretch through a diversity of thinkers from John Dewey to George Orwell and from Leonard Hobhouse to Richard Hoggart. They have of course differed in their concerns and passions, but to all of them a free society was more than the freedom to work or starve or more recently consume. This tradition offers a different understanding of freedom than that which simply assumes it is the ability to become wealthy or indeed simply to do what you like without interference. Here I have offered a historical critique of the dominant values of mainstream society rather than simply describing the transition of one way of thinking about freedom to another. Of course social reality is never that simple and social liberalism or democratic socialism continues to be part of our culture. However, it seems to me at least, that these values are currently under attack.

Of course there will be many readers of this book who may not share these values. They may either think all of this talk of freedom is simply bunkum and that we would be better off without it. They prefer instead other values like happiness or security. Freedom for them offers little other than constant questioning or uncertainty. Others may argue that they enjoy being consumers and think that choice, fun and the thrill of the purchase offers more than anything that I have mentioned. This is not merely a difference of opinion, but one where people genuinely choose different values from the ones that I am advocating. Of course I could point to the consequences of these arguments. Is a life without freedom actually worth living? If we are not free to become ourselves in a meaningful way what does that say about us as human beings? Further, what of the high cost of consumer lifestyles, often paid for by the poor of the planet or the ecological devastation it leaves in its wake? Here I make these arguments not because I think we are liberal socialists by nature, but that on balance these views and values have historically been on the right side of the argument, rejecting both neo-liberalism and more authoritarian regimes. The version of freedom defended here is not utopian ushering in a perfect society, but is historically realisable. It may of course be argued that the golden age of liberal socialism has passed and we now have to adapt to more market-driven societies with good reason due to the financial and debt crisis and the rise of global competition. The tradition of social liberalism will have to adapt itself to new sociological realities, but this does not change the guiding principles of a good (or at least) better society. This is, however, a value judgment with which the reader is free to disagree.

Freedom is less about the removal of external constraints than about understanding the wider society and historical change. Freedom is also less an abstract set of principles than it is having access to a historical narrative. The idea of freedom is intimately related to our ability to tell a story about who we are, what traditions are important, and where we are currently headed. If liberalism is a tradition it is one that needs to be able to tell a story about history. Too much time has been spent by political theorists arguing in esoteric debates of which the public can make little sense. Who on reading much liberal philosophy is inspired to take up the banner of freedom? Not really that many is my fear. The principles at stake are of course important, but they need to be attached to an ability to tell a story about our current identities. If our story about freedom is changing (as I fear it is) we need to be able to understand how this is as much a philosophical problem as it is a sociological and historical one. Part of the narrative about freedom needs to be a story we can tell about the arrival of a consumer society that has implications for the ways in which many people view freedom and their own identities. If this society began to emerge in the 1950s it is crucially related to the impact of credit cards, suburban living, the conversion of the home into a leisure centre, the rise of technological culture and of course the dominance of television and privatised living. If we add into this picture neo-liberalism and globalisation it is not surprising that our shared ideas of freedom have altered. We might also add into this context more contemporary fears about fundamentalism and political indifference. If a world of passionate ethnic belonging is one threat to a diverse society, then fundamentalism of various kinds is another. How can we guard ourselves against the threats of consumerist indifference and exclusive tribalism? Of course we may not be able to do so but, rather than trusting in the innate good sense of our fellow citizens or shrugging our shoulders, part of the answer might lie within a genuinely civic education.

The idea of a civic education is not to indoctrinate children into becoming good social liberals. It is instead the need to provide an education that emphasises the virtues of freedom. The idea of citizenship being based upon the idea of virtue can be traced back of course to the

Ancient Greeks in general and Aristotle in particular. Stressing the virtues of freedom emphasises what it is good to become. The virtuous citizen is not only good but someone who knows how to act in different situations. The danger here is that the idea of the virtuous citizen simply becomes (as indeed it was in Ancient Greece) a way for the middle classes to feel superior. This is indeed a distinct possibility, but it depends upon the skilful ability of educators to make sure this does not happen. Further, such an argument is clearly objectionable as citizens should be free to become other kinds of being. Many of our citizens will remain indifferent to matters of public concern, preferring instead to interest themselves in other activities. The idea is, however, to gently consider how the virtues of freedom might be fostered, not to impose them in an authoritarian manner. Citizens of a particular community will continue to hold a diversity of views. Another argument might be that in terms of offering a civic education we need to be entirely 'neutral' as to the loyalties displayed by our students as long as they are in keeping with the rule of law. It is not for the state or any other body to prejudice the minds of the young on contentious questions. The problem here is that there is no such thing as a neutral society. Our languages, histories, family backgrounds and broader cultural traditions have already been selected for us. Moreover it is better to be honest and admit that states and modern economies require citizens to be loyal, have a sense of connection to the host society and aim to make something of themselves. If we admit all of this (as I think we must) we are already a long way from neutrality. Finally, others might think that freedom can be simply left to itself in republics based upon equal rights and the rule of law. Recalling John Dewey (1977) we might be born relational beings but we only become members of democratic communities by learning how to. Indeed, if civic citizenship depends upon rights, responsibilities and a sense of belonging, then it needs to be more than a common set of procedures. Freedom needs to become an actual practice whereby new citizens learn to test their ideas, opinions and concerns against others. This can only be achieved by having the confidence to think for oneself, being creative, voicing concerns and acquiring the skilled art of listening. Freedom requires the practice of democratic dialogue. This practice is as much about living in a family as it is about living in a community.

Today, however, we are more aware than Dewey of living within diverse communities where there are plural ideas of the good life. Communities are increasingly plural in terms of their religious and ethnic composition. What is called for here is the ability (as I have termed it) to cross over cultural borders, challenging the imagination to think differently. If liberal societies of the past assumed a deferential population that was relatively homogenous this is no longer the case. The civic ability to think across diversity while respecting others is an essential skill in the context of modern globalised societies. The civic capacity required here is the ability to negotiate and live with difference while also being tolerant. As Dewey well understood this can really only be achieved in the context of diverse schools that reflect the general make-up of the community. This means an education where citizens of different class, ethnic and other backgrounds are mixed together. Schools have a responsibility to provide an education that enables students to become curious about one another while respecting one another's often complex identities. This requires skilful handling, but on the whole maintains a certain optimism about the capacity of young citizens to debate, learn and criticise in common settings.

The ability to deliberate on matters of common concern is not something that is easy to learn. Many citizens become anxious when they are not sure what to think. Young people lacking in personal confidence may indeed feel overwhelmed by such a requirement. However, the ability to genuinely think for oneself is a skill only learned over a number of years and requires a persistent effort. Surely it could be argued that schools are already burdened enough having to teach basic literacy and other skills, and in an evermore competitive world many parents have not surprisingly become increasingly focused on exam performance. Education for upward mobility, however, as I have already pointed out, has done a great deal of violence to its practice. If freedom is as much of a story as it is a practice, then we need locations where the skills and knowledge associated with this ideal can be passed on. This will mean that children will need to learn about different political traditions, artistic ideas and social movements that have made an impact upon their communities. This is a historical story, but it is also one that faces contemporary realities where schools provide space for a diversity of ideas and debates. This kind of civic learning will inevitably need to be joined up across the curriculum and provide a sense of the sheer diversity of different civil groups and campaigns that go on within any community.

The other main place we might gain access to critical narratives on questions of freedom is through the media of mass communication. As I have already indicated, I am concerned about the decline of public media and its replacement by communication mainly geared to selling spaces to advertisers, product placement, celebrity endorsement and the promotion of consumerism, though many European societies still have broadcasting systems that are regulated in the public interest. We might remember that during the 1960s many critical intellectuals saw the arrival of the television age as offering new possibilities for civic engagement. Public service broadcasting suggested something more than commercialism for the masses and high culture for elites. Freedom requires narratives and stories about the issues of the day that cross the class borders making provocative, popular and sometimes radical programming. Many progressives now pin their hopes on the Internet in mobilising political sentiment. This is not surprising given the increased dominance of commercial television. Indeed, recent protests have demonstrated the ability of new media to offer alternative forms of communication, though, as I have indicated, there are limits to this view. Many ordinary people's experience is still more defined by mainstream media than alternative web pages. Television in this regard still retains a considerable amount of potential to explore public concerns that are currently underutilised. Rather than retreat into the radical enclave, those concerned with freedom need to be making provocative documentaries, arresting drama and other challenging forms of public art in ways that draw together diverse audiences. Public media continues to have an important role to play in providing a source of critical reflections on public questions and issues.

Diverse narratives of freedom need to be located in the earth of our common culture. Unless they find a place to grow in our schools, universities and through our media they are likely to be driven out by an economic and political system that can easily accommodate itself with weak citizenship. The social citizenship that emerged after 1945 sought to promote an inclusive society based on freedom and responsibility. This was a citizenship of egalitarian principles that after the 1960s progressively expanded seeking to accommodate a diversity of communities and interests. Liberal institutions such as the BBC and the comprehensive school system imperfectly sought to provide zones of contact where people from different social and economic backgrounds might develop common interests and associations. These institutions (in theory at least) sought to develop a concern with the common freedom enjoyed by everyone in the community. Of course there were problems but this was a period of hope and common endeavour. But this period now seems to be passing as we turn into a more individualistic age where freedom is no longer seen as being part of the common good but becomes increasingly bound up with ideas like 'choice' and consumerism. This helps promote less than civic cultures where citizens no longer have the common meeting points to help translate a diversity of experience. The dominance of capitalism based upon class division and consumerism will always mean freedom for the powerful rather than the weak. But freedom's call remains strong and could yet take on a more subversive turn in increasingly divided communities that are based more and more frequently on freedom for the few rather than the many. As the Italian liberal socialist Carlo Rosselli (1994) argues it remains the project of the labour movement to democratise liberalism. This is a world where citizens are able to live in freedom no longer enslaved by poverty or the demands of their employers. A society where we are all free to become ourselves, find our voices and collectively participate in the discovery of the common good.

BIBLIOGRAPHY

Anderson, P. (2009) *The New Old World*, London, Verso

Arendt, H. (1958) *The Human Condition*, Chicago, IL, University of Chicago Press

—— (1961) *Between Past and Future*, London, Penguin

—— (1990) *On Revolution*, London, Penguin

—— (2000) 'Total Domination', in Baehr, P. (ed.) *The Portable Arendt*, London, Penguin Books, pp. 119–46

Aron, R. (1970) *An Essay on Freedom*, New York, World Publishers

Barstow, S. (1964) *A Kind of Loving*, London, Black Swan

Bauman, Z. (1998) *Freedom*, Milton Keynes, Open University Press

—— (2000) *Liquid Modernity*, Cambridge, Polity Press

—— (2006) *Liquid Fear*, Cambridge, Polity Press

—— (2009) *Does Ethics Have a Chance In a World of Consumers?*, Cambridge, MA, Harvard University Press

Beck, U. (1998) *Democracy Without Enemies*, Cambridge, Polity Press

—— (2006) *Cosmopolitan Vision*, Cambridge, Polity Press

Berlin, I. (1959) *'Two Concepts of Liberty': Four Essays on Liberty*, Oxford, Oxford University Press

Bernstein, R. J. (2005) *The Abuse of Evil: The Corruption of Politics and Religion Since 9/11*, Cambridge, Polity Press

Birnbaum, N. (2001) *After Progress*, Oxford, Oxford University Press

Boal, I., Clark, T.J., Matthews, J., Watts, M. (2005) *Afflicted Powers: Capital and Spectacle in a New Age of War*, London, Verso

Bobbio, N. (1996) *The Age of Rights*, Cambridge, Polity Press

Bourdieu, P. (2003) *Firing Back: Against the Tyranny of the Market 2*, London, Verso

Buck-Morss, S. (2003) *Thinking Past Terror*, London, Verso

Calhoun, C. (2007) *Nations Matter: Culture, History, and the Cosmopolitan Dream*, London, Routledge

Castells, M. (2009) *Communication Power*, Oxford, Oxford University Press

Castoriadis, C. (1991) *Philosophy, Politics, Autonomy*, Oxford, Oxford University Press

Crick, B. (2007) '*Nineteen Eighty-Four*: Context and Controversey', in Rodden, J. (ed.) *The Cambridge Companion to George Orwell*, Cambridge, Cambridge University Press, pp. 146–59

Decker, J. (2004) *Ideology*, London, Palgrave

Dewey, J. (1977) 'Search for the Great Community', in Sidorsky, D. (ed.) *John Dewey: The Essential Writings*, New York, Harper Row, pp. 13–22

Ehrenreich, B. (2010) *Smile or Die*, London, Granta

Elias, N. (1988) 'The Retreat of Sociologists Into The Present', in Gouldsblom, J. and Mennell, S. (eds) *The Norbert Elias Reader*, Oxford, Blackwell

Falk, R. (2000) *Human Rights Horizons*, London, Routledge

Foucault, M. (1984a) 'What is Enlightenment?', in *The Foucault Reader*, London, Penguin

—— (1984b) *The History of Sexuality, Vol. 3: The Care of the Self*, London, Penguin

Frankl, V. (1964) *Man's Search for Meaning*, London, Hodder and Stoughton

Fromm, E. (1941) *Escape from Freedom*, New York, Avon Books

—— (1995) '*On the Art of Living': The Essential Fromm*, London, Constable, pp. 15–19

Giddens, A. (1992) *Modernity and Self-Identity*, Cambridge, Polity Press

—— (1998) *The Third Way*, Cambridge, Polity Press

—— (2007) *Europe in the Global Age*, Cambridge, Polity Press

Giroux, H. (1993) 'Literacy and the Politics of Difference', in Lankshear, C. and McLaren, P. (eds) *Critical Literacy: Politics, Praxis, and the Postmodern*, Albany, State University of New York Press, pp. 367–78

—— (2006) 'Cultural Studies, Critical Pedagogy, and the Responsibility of Intellectuals', in C.G. Robbins (ed.) *The Giroux Reader*, London, Paradigm Publishers, pp. 47–66

Gramsci, A. (1988) *A Gramsci Reader*, London, Lawrence and Wishart

Gray, J. (2007) *Black Mass: Apocalyptic Religion and the Death of Utopia*, London, Penguin

Habermas, J. (2001) *The Postnational Constellation*, Cambridge, Polity Press

—— and Derrida, J. (2003) 'February 15, or What Binds Europeans Together: A Plea for a Common Foreign Policy, Beginning in the Core of Europe', *Constellations* 10(3), pp. 291–97

Hamilton, C. (2004) *Growth Fetish*, London, Pluto Press

Harvey, D. (2005) *A Brief History of Neoliberalism*, Oxford, Oxford University Press

Hasan, M. (2010) 'The Torturer's Apprentices', *New Statesman*, 22 February, p. 16

Hobhouse, L.T. (1964) *Liberalism*, Oxford, Oxford University

Hoggart, R. (1957) *The Uses of Literacy*, London, Chatto and Windus

—— (1970) *Speaking to Each Other*, London, Pelican

hooks, b. (2004) *The Will to Change: Men, Masculinity and Love*, New York, Washington Square Press

Jenkins, H. (2004) 'The Cultural Logic of Media Convergence', *International Journal of Cultural Studies* 7(1), pp. 33–43

Judt, T. (2010) *Ill Fares the Land*, London, Allen Lane

Keane, J. (2009) *The Life and Death of Democracy*, London, Simon and Schuster

Klein, N. (2007) *The Shock Doctrine: The Rise of Disaster Capitalism*, London, Allen Lane

Layard, R. (2005) *Happiness: Lessons from a New Science*, London, Penguin

Marcuse, H. (1972) *One Dimensional Man*, London, Abacus

Mill, J.S. (1924) *Autobiography*, London, Open University Press

—— (1974) *On Liberty*, London, Penguin

Mosse, G.L. (1978) *Toward the Final Solution: A History of European Racism*, London, J.M. Dent and Sons Ltd

Offe, C. (2005) *Reflections on America*, Cambridge, Polity Press

Orwell, G. (1945) *Animal Farm: A Fairy Story*, London, Secker and Warberg

—— (1953) *Such, Such Were the Joys*, London, Harcourt Brace and Company

—— (1968a) 'Not Counting Niggers', in *The Collected Essays, Journalism and Letters of George Orwell, Vol. 1: An Age Like This, 1920–1940*, Harmondsworth, Penguin, pp. 434–38

—— (1968b) 'Letter to Francis A. Henson (extract)', in *The Collected Essays, Journalism and Letters of George Orwell, Vol. 4: In Front of Your Nose, 1945–1950*, Harmondsworth, Penguin Books, p. 502

—— (1968c) 'Inside the Whale', in *The Collected Essays, Journalism and Letters of George Orwell, Vol. 1: An Age Like This, 1920–1940*, Harmondsworth, Penguin Books, pp. 540–77

—— (1968d) 'As I Please 34', in *The Collected Essays, Journalism and Letters of George Orwell, Vol. 3: As I Please, 1943–1945*, Harmondsworth, Penguin, pp. 158–61

—— (1968e) 'Why I Write', in *The Collected Essays, Journalism and Letters of George Orwell, Vol. 1: An Age Like This, 1920–1940*, Harmondsworth, Penguin, pp. 23–30

—— (1968f) 'Notes on Nationalism', in *The Collected Essays, Journalism and Letters of George Orwell, Vol. 3: As I Please, 1943–1945*, Harmondsworth, Penguin, pp. 410–31

—— (1968g) 'Towards European Unity', in *The Collected Essays, Journalism and Letters of George Orwell, Vol. 4: In Front of Your Nose, 1945–1950*, Harmondsworth, Penguin, pp. 423–29

—— (1999) *Nineteen Eighty-Four*, London, Secker and Warberg

—— (2001a) 'As I Please 56 [On European Freedom]', Tribune, 26 January, 1945' in Davison, P. (ed.) *Orwell and Politics*, London, Penguin, pp. 348–51

—— (2001b) *The Road to Wigan Pier*, London, Penguin

—— (2001c) 'The Intellectual Revolt: Four Articles, Manchester Evening News', in Davison, P. (ed.) *Orwell and Politics*, London, Penguin, pp. 415–38

Patterson, O. (1991) *Freedom, Vol. 1: Freedom in the Making of Western Culture*, London, I.B. Tauris and Co. Ltd

Pieterse, J.N. (2004) *Globalization or Empire*, London, Routledge

Poggi, G. (1972) *Images of Society: Essays on the Sociological Theories of Tocqueville, Marx, and Durkheim*, Palo Alto, CA, Stanford University Press

Putnam, R. (2000) *Bowling Alone: The Collapse and Renewal of American Community*, New York, Touchstone Books

Ricoeur, P. (1996) 'Reflections on a new ethos for Europe' in Kearney, R. (ed.) *The Hermeneutics of Action*, London, Sage

—— (2007) *The Just*, Chicago, Chicago University

Rifkin, J. (2004) *The European Dream*, Cambridge, Polity Press

Rose, J. (2001) *The Intellectual Life of the British Working Classes*, New Haven, CT, and London, Yale University Press

Rosselli, C. (1994) *Liberal Socialism*, Princeton, NJ, Princeton University Press

Rustin, M. (2007a) '*The Long Revolution* Revisited', *Soundings* 35, pp. 16–30

—— (2007b) 'What's Wrong with Happiness', *Soundings* 36, pp. 67–84

Said, E. (1994) *Representations of the Intellectual: The 1993 Reith Lectures*, London, Vintage

—— (2004) *Humanism and Democratic Criticism*, London, Palgrave

Schell, J. (2003) *The Unconquerable World*, London, Penguin

Short, C. (2004) *An Honourable Deception: New Labour, Iraq and the Misuse of Power*, London, Free Press

Starr, P. (2007) *Freedom's Power: The History and Promise of Liberalism*, New York, Basic Books

Tawney, R.H. (1961) *The Acquisitive Society*, London, Collins

—— (1964) *The Radical Tradition*, London, Penguin Books

Taylor, C. (1982) 'The Diversity of Goods', in Sen, A. and Williams, B. (eds) *Utilitarianism and Beyond*, Cambridge, Cambridge University Press, pp. 129–44

—— (1989) 'Marxism and Socialist Humanism', in Archer, R. (ed.) *Out of Apathy: Voices of the New Left 30 Years On*, London, Verso, pp. 59–80

—— (1991) *The Malaise of Modernity*, Canada, Anansi

Thompson, E.P. (1970) *Writing By Candelight*, London, Merlin Press

—— (1978) *The Poverty of Theory*, London, Merlin Press

de Tocqueville, A. (1998) *Democracy in America*, London, Wordsworth

Todorov, T. (2003) *Hope and Memory*, London, Atlantic Books

—— (2009) *In Defence of the Enlightenment*, London, Atlantic Books

—— (2010a) *The Fear of Barbarians*, Cambridge, Polity Press

—— (2010b) *Torture and the War on Terror*, London and New York, Seagull Books

Tressell, R. (2005) *The Ragged Trousered Philanthropists*, Oxford, Oxford University Press

Wilkinson, R. and Pickett, K. (2009) *The Spirit Level*, London, Allen Lane

Williams, R. (1962) *Border Country*, London, Chatto and Windus

—— (1965) *The Long Revolution*, London, Pelican

—— (1980) *Culture and Materialism*, London, Verso

—— (1984) *Orwell*, London, Flamingo

—— (1989) *Resources of Hope*, London, Verso

INDEX

Abu Graib 40
activists 61
Afghanistan war 39
American revolution 10–11
Ancient Greece 7–9, 20, 74;
    philosophers 8
Anderson, P. 68
Animal Farm (Orwell) 3
anti-slavery movement 12
Arab Spring 1
Arendt, H. 8, 10, 14, 17, 20, 28,
    34–5
Aristotle 8, 74
Aron, R. 12
art 17, 18
authoritarianism 15, 16, 26, 41, 43;
    regimes 1, 3, 14
autonomy 8–9, 11

Barstow, S. 54, 55
Bauman, Z. 8, 33
BBC 33
Beck, U. 34, 64
Berlin, I. 13–14
Berlin Wall: fall (1989) 46
Bernstein, R. 39
Big Brother (TV series) 36
Big Brother society 24–43;
    democratic pedagogy 41–3;
    neo-liberalism and cultural politics
    37–43; new media age 31–7

Birnbaum, N. 69
black politics 54
Blair, Prime Minister 'Tony' 40
Bobbio, N. 60
Border Country (Williams) 56
Bourdieu, P. 21, 68
Britain 33, 47
Buck-Mors, S. 39
Bush doctrine 38

Calhoun, C. 63
capitalism 12, 17–18, 21, 29–30,
    32, 37–8, 47, 51, 53, 77
Castells, M. 31–3
Castoriadis, C. 8
celebrities 1
Chicago school of economics 38
Chile 37
Christianity 14
citizen–journalist 32
citizens 2, 15, 22, 24, 29–30, 45,
    48–9, 61, 74; new media 31–3
citizenship 48–9, 51, 62–6, 69, 76;
    global 61, 63
civic freedom 14, 44
civic humanism 10–14, 16
civic participation 10–12;
    decline 22
civil institutions 45
civil society 32, 49, 61
climate change 61

Cold War 25–6
collectivism 47
commercial corporations 57
common will 11
communication 17, 33, 76;
   new technology 31–3
communism 25
community 13–14, 16–18, 61, 75–7;
   inclusion 49–50
consumerism 15, 34–7, 57, 77;
   society 3, 15, 34, 73
control society 35–6
cosmopolitan freedom 59–70;
   politics and spectacle 68–70
cultural differences 56
cultural freedom: educated liberal
   socialism 52–6; third way liberal
   socialism 47–51; *X Factor*
   education 56–8
cultural production 17, 32
culture 16–17, 21, 31, 35, 56–7, 72,
   76; democratic 39–40;
   entrepreneurial 35; market-based
   35, 57–8; politics 37–43

Decker, J. 29
democracy 3, 6–7, 10–12, 15–16,
   18, 35, 39–40, 62, 66; Blair–Bush
   years 40; critique necessity 40;
   'democratising' 49
democratic egalitarianism 52
democratic socialism 16, 18, 41
Derrida, J. 67
Dewey, J. 74–5
dictatorship 9; *see also* totalitarianism
Disney 57
dissent 32, 40
'doublethink' 38, 40

economy 16, 29, 35, 53, 63;
   knowledge and information 48,
   50; low-wage 68
education 3–4, 17–18, 29–30, 35,
   42, 46, 50–1, 55, 73–6; media
   56–8; system reform 52–3
Elias, N. 4

elites 18, 21, 68; corporate 35
empire politics 37
Enlightenment 9–10, 21; critique 19
equality 11, 14, 22, 45, 49
ethical sensibility 20
ethics 20, 22–3
Europe 2, 11, 45–6, 53–4, 60, 63–9
European Convention of Human
   Rights (1950) 64
European Union (EU) 68
exploitation 41

Falk, R. 60
fame 36
fascism 28, 42
fear 34
feminism 54
formal freedoms 12, 14
Foucault, M. 19, 20
Frankl, V. 23
free will 14
free-market reforms 37–8, 46
freedom: 1960's 47; codifying
   19–20; definition 7, 19–20, 43;
   idea 4, 71; plurality 12; values 2,
   6–23; *see also* unfreedom
'freedom's children' 34
French revolution 10
Friedman, M. 38
Fromm, E. 15, 36

Giddens, A. 48–50, 61, 67
Giroux, H. 42, 55
globalisation 48
good society 59
Gray, J. 47
Greece *see* Ancient Greece
Guantanamo Bay 40

Habermas, J. 66–7
happiness and freedom 6–23;
   freedom histories 7–13; liberalism
   13–16; postmodernism and
   neo-liberalism 18–21; 'the long
   revolution' 16–18
Hasan, M. 40

hierarchies 2
history 3–4, 7–13, 66, 73
Hobhouse, L. 44, 45
Hoggart, R. 52, 69
hooks, bell 27
human rights 20, 37–8, 41, 60–4;
   abuse 37–8; universal 9, 60

identity 4, 20, 63, 65; civic 3
ideology 3, 29–31
individualism 12, 13, 20, 36, 50–1
inequality 10, 21, 50
institution-building 66–7
intellectuals 25, 64, 67–8, 76;
   democratic role 42
Internet 31–2, 76
Iraq war 37, 39, 60, 67

Jenkins, H. 32
Judt, T. 45
justice 41, 42

Keane, J. 39
A Kind of Loving (Barstow) 54
Klein, N. 37

labour movement 4, 18, 52, 77
language 3, 63; of evil 39
law 45, 61
Lenin, Vladimir 10
liberal democracies 29, 30
liberal institutions 77
liberal socialism 44–8, 57; educated
   52–6; third way 47–51
liberalism 13–16, 69–70, 71–2;
   development 15; progressive 68;
   see also neo-liberalism
liberty 13–14, 41–2, 44–5

Marcuse, H. 29, 30
the market 15, 29–30, 35, 53, 57–8;
   free-market reforms 37–8, 46
market crash (2008) 50
market freedom 21, 45, 59
market society 30, 35, 60
Marxism 12

media 3–4, 56–8, 61, 69–70, 76;
   networked 32; new age 31–7;
   'old' 31
Middle East 1
middle-class 50
Mill, J. 13, 14, 45
modernity 6–7, 17, 29
morality 47
Mosse, G. 9

narrative hospitality 65
nation states 59–70
nationalism 63–4, 68
negative liberty 13–14
neo-liberalism 7, 18–21, 34, 37–43,
   67, 69, 71; market reforms 46;
   see also liberalism
network society 31–2
new economic order 53
New Left 45
new media 31–7, 76
New Right 46
Nineteen Eighty-Four (Orwell) 24,
   26–8, 31, 37; Central Party 26–7,
   37; meaning 26–8; O'Brien 27–8;
   plot 26–7; Winston Smith 26–8
North America 2, 45–7, 54,
   63–4, 69

oppression 7–9, 11
Orwell, George 3, 23, 24–43, 63–4
the Other 19–20, 33, 66

patriarchy 27
Patterson, O. 7–8
pedagogy: democratic 41–3
personal freedom 14, 15, 34–5
philosophy 19
Pieterse, J. 38
politics 21, 26, 60, 62, 66–7, 68–70;
   cultural 37–43; ideologies 3;
   institutions 11; Left-wing 21,
   45–8
the poor 49–50
post-structuralism 19
postmodernism 18–21

poverty 10, 42
propaganda 26–7, 36
public freedom 34–5
public space 34–5, 37
Putnam, R. 22

racism 9
The Ragged Trousered Philanthropist (Tressell) 53
Reagan, President Ronald 46
Ricoeur, P. 57, 65–6
Rifkin, J. 67
Right-wing politics 26, 46–8
Romantics 14
Rose, J. 51
Rosselli, C. 77
Rousseau, J. 10–11
Russian revolution 10
Rustin, M. 22

Said, E. 25
Schell, J. 37
schools 52, 75, 77
secret state 33
security 3; state 33–4, 41
self-government 49
The Shock Doctrine (Klein) 37
Short, C. 40
slavery 7–8, 11–12, 15
social democracy 47–8
social liberalism 69–70, 71–2
social movements 19, 32–3
social standing 12
social state 16
socialism 18, 26, 42, 44–5, 64
society 2–4, 6–23, 30–2, 35–6, 44, 59–61, 73; autonomous 8; Big Brother 24–43; competition 21; democratic 6, 12–13, 15–16, 18; free 72; reproduction 4
sociology 2–4
Soviet Union 64
Spanish civil war 42
Starr, P. 15
the state 33, 35, 49, 59–70; communication power 33;

controlled nations 30; image promotion 36; policy 35

Tawney, R. 50–1
Taylor, C. 10, 14, 22–3
technology 50; new forms 31–3
television 33, 56, 69, 76; talent shows 36, 56–8
Thatcher, Prime Minister Margaret 46
Thompson, E. 25, 33
thought control 29, 30, 37
de Tocqueville, A. 10–12, 13, 22
Todorov, T. 9, 40, 64–5
torture 37, 38, 40
totalitarianism 11, 14, 22, 28, 34, 39, 42, 46, 60; society 11, 22
Tressell, R. 53, 54
tyranny 12

unemployment 41
unfreedom 15, 30, 34–6, 53, 57; society 30
United Kingdom (UK) 33, 47
United States of America (USA) 10–12, 39, 60, 67–9; aggression 67
Universal Declaration of Human Rights (1948) 60
utilitarianism 22–3

values 2–3, 72; Victorian 47
victimhood 66
virtue and freedom 71–7

war 37, 38
'war on terror' 37–41, 67–8
Washington 37
Washington Consensus 60
Watkins, G. 27
the wealthy 49–50
the West 1–2, 20, 45–6; modernity 6–7, 29; society 2, 7, 23
Williams, R. 16–18, 36, 38, 56
working-class 51; fiction 53–5; movement 44–5, 53

youth 57; education 52